MILITARY SWORDS OF JAPAN
1868–1945

The authors

Richard Fuller, aged 40, lives in Bristol, England, with his wife and two children. A drainage engineer by profession, he maintains an interest in all branches of militaria collecting and started concentrating on Japanese military swords in 1972; he is currently a member of the To-ken Society of Great Britain and the Japanese Sword Society of the United States. He and Ron Gregory have previously collaborated on three limited-edition books on Showa period swordsmiths and oshigata (tang rubbings).

Ron Gregory is retired and lives with his wife near Bedford, England. He started collecting just after the Second World War, becoming a part-time sword and militaria dealer and a founder-member of the Arts Circle affiliated to the Japan Society of London. His extensive collections of Japanese and ethnological weapons have been used to illustrate many books and articles, as well as his own works. In 1971, he became the first person to publish an English-language booklet on Japanese military swords. He is also currently a member of the To-ken Society of Great Britain and the Japanese Society of the United States.

Cover photograph

Left to right

An officers' shin-guntō with a general officers' tassel. Dating from the period of the Second World War, the sword has a blade by Kazusada, *c.*1490.

An army company officers' kyu-guntō, with an unsigned blade and a field officers' tassel of *c.*1937–45.

An 1873/4 pattern naval officers' kyu-guntō. The blade is signed NAOTAKA, *c.*1865.

A naval officers' kyu-guntō of the pattern *c.*1914. Its blade is signed SUKESADA and dated 1579.

(All from the R. Gregory collection.)

RICHARD FULLER AND RON GREGORY

MILITARY SWORDS OF JAPAN 1868-1945

Line drawings by Richard Fuller

ARMS AND
ARMOUR

First published in Great Britain in 1986 by
Arms and Armour Press, an imprint of Cassell Plc,
Villiers House,
41–47 Strand,
London WC2N 5JE

Reprinted 1987
Reprinted 1988, 1989, 1990

Distributed in the USA by
Sterling Publishing Co. Inc.,
387 Park Avenue South,
New York, NY 10016–8810

Distributed in Australia by
Capricorn Link (Australia) Pty Ltd,
P.O.Box 665, Lane Cove,
New South Wales 2066, Australia.

British Library Cataloguing in Publication Data

Fuller, Richard
    Military Swords of Japan, 1868–1945.
    1. Swords—Japan—History—19th century
    2. Swords—Japan—History—20th century
    I. Title   II. Gregory, Ron
    739.7'22'0952   NK6784

    ISBN 0-85368-796-X

Edited and designed by John Walter
Typeset by Typesetters (Birmingham) Limited
Smethwick, West Midlands
Printed and bound by The Bath Press

Contents

Acknowledgements

The authors wish to express their thanks to all those who provided the assistance and information which made the preparation of this book possible. Special acknowledgement must go to: B. W. Robinson for continued assistance and a wealth of knowledge. Han Bing Siong and Brenton Williams for the use of photographs of their excellent collections and additional information. Roy Norwood and – especially – John Holden for their time and effort in taking photographs for this book. Ken Gilborson of Gilborson Brothers, Photographers, Kingswood, Bristol.

John Penny for continued encouragement.

The Imperial War Museum, West Point Military Academy Museum and the US Naval Academy Museum for use of their photographs.

Fred L. Honeycutt, Jr, for much information on arsenal marks.

C. Halvorson, Keith Hostler, Gary Murtha, James Silver, Clarence Siman, Fred Stephens, Yoshinobu Sugiyama, George Trotter, Peter Yorke, Roy Lindus and Mick Davis.

The wives of the authors, Idwen and Betty, for their forbearance during the time-consuming research and preparation of this project.

Satsuma rebel samurai, 1877.

An army first lieutenant, 1871.

An army second lieutenant in parade dress, 1873.

Introduction

> JUST AS THE CHERRY BLOSSOM FADES
> AND FALLS TO THE GROUND, SO IT IS WITH MY USEFUL LIFE.
> SHOULD IT PROVE TO BE OF USE TO MY EMPEROR
> I WOULD NOT FAIL TO FALL.
>
> *A poem on a military sword blade*

Until quite recently, it has been believed that Japanese military swords are no more than curios seized from a nation defeated in the Second World War. It was even some time before it was realised that such swords could be found with old hand-forged blades. The market for genuine samurai swords (wazikashi, katana, tachi) has grown rapidly to a point where they are beyond the financial resources of the average collector. Thus, military swords have become a popular substitute and even those with machine-made blades successfully command high prices.

Unfortunately, the upswing in demand has not been met with an increase in published reference material. To date, only one English-language book has dealt specifically with military swords of 1868–1945 – *Japanese Military Swords* by R. Gregory, published in 1971 but no longer available. Traditional samurai swords have been well researched, in both Japanese and English, but the military patterns – if they are mentioned at all – are covered briefly or dismissively.

In January 1868, the ruling Tokugawa-clan shoguns (or 'military rulers') were overthrown by a coalition of the powerful clans in the south-west and the imperial court in Kyōto. The emperor, Mutsuhito, though aged only fifteen, soon re-established imperial rule in his new capital – Yedō, which had been renamed Tōkyō.

European countries were already carving up China by bribery and coercion to obtain lucrative trading empires. Japan, with an isolationist policy and feudal traditions, was ripe for similar treatment unless the danger was foreseen, and trade and defences modernised. Rapid changes occurred under Mutsuhito and his cabinet. Centuries-old feudal customs were abolished and foreign instructors, both military and industrial, arrived to enable Japan to take a place in the modern world.

Among the first to suffer was the privileged samurai class. Compulsory wearing of swords by samurai was made optional in 1871, as was the cutting of hair. Withdrawn, too, was a samurai's right to kill a commoner for any insult – real or imaginary. On 1 January 1877 the Haitorei edict of 1876 came into effect, restricting wearing of swords to just the military and police in uniform. Apparently, this order was subsequently repealed but, by then, samurai society had vanished for ever.

No sword with a blade made after 1877 can be called 'samurai', as that warrior class had ceased to exist. Swordsmiths lost their trade, often turning to cutlery manufacture, and many of their best skills died out. It is said that not all have been rediscovered, even by the best 20th-century masters.

In 1867, France was regarded as the greatest military power in Europe and French instructors were imported to create the new Japanese army – officered with ex-samurai at the beginning, but later by commoners. French influence had a lasting affect on the design of full-dress uniforms.

After the French defeat by Germany during the Franco-Prussian War (1870–71), German instructors were brought in until, in turn, they were withdrawn in 1894.

As far as Japanese swords are concerned, foreign influence may be seen in the angled pommel, the handguard and the knucklebow common on French and German swords.

Until the late 1860s, army-orientated Japan had no navy of any strength. To protect trade and guard against European naval power, the Japanese soon needed to build up their own naval forces on Western lines. British instructors and vessels were employed. Naval uniforms were based on the contemporary British patterns but, except for a very early influence, naval swords followed the general European design.

The spectacular rise of both army and navy power culminated in the defeat of a major European nation, Russia, in 1905. The destruction of the Russian Pacific and Baltic fleets and the successful conquest of Manchuria underscored Japan's claims as a world power.

An army artillery NCO, 1886.

TWENTIETH-CENTURY SWORDS

The first military swords are virtually indistinguishable from their European counterparts. Their blades were originally mass-produced but, because they were found unsuitably flexible and weak by officers with kendō training, a return to traditional manufacturing methods and blade styles was made around 1900. Sword hilts incorporated knucklebows until the 1930s, when the traditionally styled 'shin-guntō' was introduced. A naval version or 'kai-guntō' was also prescribed. Both types are erroneously called 'samurai swords' by the layman, although more than three-quarters of them have blades made after 1926 (i.e., Shōwa period).

Officers could, if they wished, have their military-pattern swords (guntō) mounted with old ancestral blades often kept as family heirlooms. Japanese regulations pertaining to military swords appear to have been particularly lax, as many variations in fittings are encountered. Even civilian katana and wakizashi, suitably protected, could be carried on active service if preferred.

Until the final surrender in 1945, an officer's sword was considered essential both as a fighting weapon – symbol of

An army officer, 1904–5.

authority over his men – and a representation of the samurai code of 'bushido'. A wartime magazine clarifies its purpose thus:

'Most Nippon warriors fighting in the present Greater East Asia war bear Nippon swords. Practically speaking, there is no need for officers of the air force, tank corps and navy to carry long swords. But . . . they carry swords not only to defend themselves against the enemy, but to bear ever in mind the warrior's code of honour.'

Most Japanese military swords encountered in the West were captured, surrendered or confiscated during the Second World War. They represent the end of a traditional veneration of the sword that had lasted over a thousand years. Many were carried and used in campaigns of extreme ferocity or hardship. Naval swords were carried aboard warships and even on midget submarines. There are many accounts of army officers, armed only with swords, attacking entrenched infantry – even tanks. Unfortunately, there is now little chance of learning the history of most of these weapons, but the strong possibility of such active service should always be borne in mind.

This book, alas, is no more than an outline of general development in 1868–1945; however, it may enable the reader to identify sword patterns and fittings that are not documented elsewhere.

So that research may continue, we would appreciate details of any unusual swords or fittings in collections. Additional information in the form of introduction dates or surrender documents is always invaluable.

RICHARD FULLER
RON GREGORY

Bristol, 1986

An army officer, 1912.
An army officer in tropical dress, 1926.
An army officer in field dress, 1938.

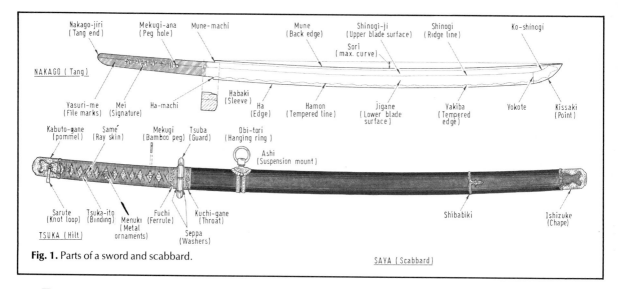

Fig. 1. Parts of a sword and scabbard.

Glossary

Before any description of Japanese swords can be given, it is important that the reader becomes familiar with the basic Japanese terminology that may be found in the text; fig. 1 illustrates the various parts of a typical Japanese military sword.

Details of the many variations in tempered edge patterns, blade sections, traditional methods of blade manufacture, etc., are covered in many of the reference books devoted to the traditional 'samurai' sword.

AIKUCHI	A dirk without a guard. See *tantō*.
AOI	The guard (*tsuba*) shape found on *shin-guntō* swords, resembling the Assarum plant.
ASHI	A scabbard band or mount for suspending a sword. The suspension ring is called an 'obi-tori'.
BUKE ZUKURI	A traditional style of sword with a tape-bound hilt, hand-forged blade and lacquered scabbard, e.g. *katana* and *wakizashi*.
DAI-SEPPA	The large washer next to the guard; one on each side.
FUCHI	The ferrule at the base of the hilt.
HABAKI	A metal collar on the blade which acts as a wedge in the scabbard.
HAMON	A misty line of martensite crystals between the *yakiba* and blade surface. May be found in many patterns, each with a name.
ISHIZUKE	The scabbard chape or drag.
KABUTŌ-GANE	The pommel of *tachi, shin-* and *kai-guntō* swords with an opening for the sword knot loop.
KAI-GUNTŌ	*Kai* (sea) – *gun* (military) – *tō* (sword): a naval sword pattern resembling the traditional *tachi*.
KASHIRA	The pommel of a civilian *katana* or *wakizashi*. A cap having the braid tied through the centre of each side but with no provision for a sword knot.
KATANA	A traditional style of long sword with a 24-30in blade, carried cutting-edge uppermost through the waist sash. See *wakizashi*.
KOGAI	The skewer or head-pin carried in a pocket of a civilian sword or dagger scabbard as a companion to the *kozuka*.

KOZUKA	A small knife carried in a pocket of a civilian sword or dagger scabbard as a companion to the *kogai*.
KURIKATA	The raised wood, horn or metal knob on a civilian scabbard to prevent it slipping through the waist sash.
KYU-GUNTŌ	*Kyu* (proto or first) – *gun* (military) – *tō* (sword): a European-style military sword, usually fitted with a hand-forged blade introduced at the beginning of the 20th century. Often referred to as a 'proto army sword'.
MACHI	A step or notch between a blade and tang.
MEI	The blade signature or inscription.
MEKUGI	A bamboo peg that secures the hilt and blade.
MEKUGI-ANA	The hole in the tang for the *mekugi*. There may be more than one.
MENUKI	A hilt ornament under the tape binding.
MON	A family badge or crest.
MUMEI	An unsigned tang.
NAGA-MARU	The ovoid *tsuba* shape found on *kai-guntō* swords.
NANAKO	A common background decoration of raised dots – resembling fishroe – found on sword mountings.
ORIGAMI	A certificate given by a panel of sword appraisers, identifying and authenticating the make of a blade together with a valuation.
OSHIGATA	A tang rubbing or 'smoke' recording the inscription.
POMMEL	See *kabutō-ganē* and *kashira*.
RIO-HITSU	The holes in the sword guard for retention clip, *kogai*, *kozuka*, etc. The tang hole is called 'nakago-ana'.
SAMĒ	Rayskin used on hilts and scabbards, characterised by rounded nodules of varying sizes. See *shagreen*.
SARU-TE	A metal or cord sword knot loop passing through the *kabutō-ganē*.
SAYA	The Japanese name for a scabbard.
SEPPA	Small guard washers. Up to three may be found on each side of the *dai-seppa*.
SHIBABIKI	An intermediate scabbard reinforcement, binding the two halves together. It was used for decorative purposes on metal military scabbards.
SHAKUDO	A gunmetal-blue finish applied to sword mountings, especially civilian examples, achieved through the patination of copper mixed with small amounts of gold.
SHAGREEN	A word of Turkish origin, used for the sharkskin found on hilts and scabbards, characterized by small diamond-shaped nodules. See *samē*.
SHIN-GUNTŌ	From *shin* (new) – *gun* (military) – *tō* (sword): the most common pattern of army sword, based on the traditional *tachi*.
TACHI	A traditional slung sword with a blade 24-30in long. The scabbard has two suspension mounts (*ashi*) to accommodate the belt hangers.
TANTŌ	A dirk fitted with a guard. See *aikuchi*.
TSUKA	The hilt of a Japanese sword.
WAKIZASHI	A traditional short sword with a 16-20in blade, carried cutting-edge uppermost through the waist sash as a companion to the *katana*. A matching pair is called a 'daishō'.
YAKIBA	The tempered blade cutting-edge bordered by the *hamon*.
YASURI-ME	Tang file marks.

SWORD PERIODS

The dating of Japanese-made swords is divided thus:

Ancient, pre-900 AD.

Kotō (old swords), 900–1596. 1596 is accepted as the most popular date, falling conveniently at the commencement of the Keichō reign-era. It was about this time that swords were confiscated from farmers and commoners. Alfred Dobrée, in *Japanese Sword Blades* (first published in 1905), uses 1603. 'This division', he says, 'was made by Taiko, Toyotomi Hideyoshi in whose times flourished the first sword expert whose judgement was accepted as infallible – named Honami Kōsetsu.' John Yumoto, in *The Samurai Sword*, specifies 1530 during the Kyōroku reign-era, but gives no reasons for his assumption.

Shintō (new swords), 1596–1800.

Shin-shintō (new-new swords), 1800–68. This period conveniently terminates at the restoration of Mutsuhito in 1868 and the beginning of the Meiji nengō. Not until 1876 was sword wear prohibited, after which the decline in blade manufacture occurred; 1876, therefore, could be preferred to 1868.

Modern swords, 1868 to date. Modern blade dating should be by the nengō: Meiji, Taishō and Shōwa – 1868–1912, 1912–26 and 1926 to date.

MODERN JAPANESE EMPERORS

The lineage of the emperors claims unbroken descent from the first emperor, Jimmu-Tennō who, it is said, founded the empire in 660 BC. On acceding to the throne, each new emperor gives his period of rule a reign-name or 'nengo' by which his supremacy is known. After his death, the emperor is also known by his nengō. Thus, Hirohito will be known as Emperor Shōwa after he dies, although the Japanese dating system in current use nonetheless relates to the Shōwa era. The periods since the restoration are:

Date	Emperor	Nengō	Characters
1868–1912	Mutsuhito	Meiji (Enlightened rule)	明 治
1912–26	Yoshihito	Taishō (Great correctness or equity)	大 正
1926–present	Hirohito	Shōwa (Radiant peace)	昭 和

Imperial line

The great Emperor Mutsuhito (known as Meiji after his death) came to the throne at the age of only 15, ruling over Japan for 45 years before dying of stomach cancer on 29 July 1912. His reign had seen Japan grow from a feudal society to a major power, expanding both industry and the armed forces, introducing western methods, clothes and materials. He was survived by only one of more than a dozen sons.

NB. In the genealogical table, only the main branches of descent are shown.

```
                                    ┌──────────── Mutsuhito ────────────┐
                                                   (Meiji)
                                            (1852–1868–1912)
    ┌───────────┬───────────┬───────────────┬───────────┬───────────┐
 Princess     Princess      Yoshihito      Princess     Princess
 Masako       Fusako         (Taishō)       Nobuko       Toshiko
 (1888–       (b. 1890)    (1879–1912–1926) (1891–1933)  (b. 1896)
 1940)        Married      Married Princess Married      Married
 Married      Prince          Fujiwara      Prince       Prince
 Prince       Kitashirakawa II              Asaka        Higashikuni
 Takeda
         ┌───────────┬───────────────┬───────────┬───────────┐
      Chichibu        Hirohito      Takamatsu    Mikasa
      Yasuhito         (Shōwa)      Nobuhito     Takahito
      (1902–1953)  (1900–1926–present) (b. 1905)  (b. 1915)
      Rival brother  Married Princess
                        Nakago
```

Rebellion swords

Plate 1. Two samurai in the transitional period, 1868. They have European clothing and, in one case, Japanese footwear. The top knot has almost disappeared and the forehead is no longer shaved. The samurai on the left carries the traditional 'daishō' or pair of swords worn through the belt. The other has only one long sword, carried by the shoulder belt or sash.

Plate 2. A wakizashi in 'rebellion' mounts of plain blackened iron. 1877. The hilt binding is canvas. The separate hilt is from a 'rebellion' katana. The black leather frog of about 1870 was for use with wakizashi or katana when carried with military uniform. (Fuller and Gregory collection.)

Always involved in Japanese expansionist policies, Korea became a source of dissention when a Japanese envoy was reported to have been insulted by the Korean court in 1872. This was regarded as a personal insult to the Emperor.

A former samurai, General Saigō Takamori, military commander-in-chief to the government, demanded to be sent to Korea to avenge the indignity or get himself killed in the process. He hoped this would precipitate a war from which Japan would emerge victorious, gaining Korea as a satellite.

Saigō was also involved in the political rivalry between his Satsuma clan and those of Choshū and Tosa. However, the government declined his offer, fearful of European military intervention and probably backed by his rivals.

Resigning in a fury, Saigō retired to Kagoshima from where — since he could not reach an amicable agreement — he planned to overthrow the government.

Assembling an army of 14,000 samurai, mostly from the student ranks of Satsuma and Ōsumi, he marched up the west coast of Kyūshū with the intention of reaching Tōkyō. The city of Kumamoto was besieged since it could not be circumvented safely, but it was eventually relieved by a government army of 30,000 conscripts under Imperial Prince Arisugawa Tarahito. The rebel army was forced towards the east coast and brought to battle at Nobeoka. The bulk of Saigō's defeated army surrendered on 9 August 1877.

Seeing defeat was inevitable, Saigō and his few remaining followers committed suicide on 24 September 1877 on Shiroyama, a hill above Kagoshima. The day of the samurai was truly over. Hei-min troops (conscripts and commoners) had justified the newly introduced military service system by defeating samurai power forever.

REBELLION SWORDS

At the beginning of the revolt, local armouries were seized by the rebels and their sword blades quickly taken to be mounted. These are known as 'Satsuma' or 'Rebellion' swords and deserve to be mentioned, although not considered strictly of military pattern.

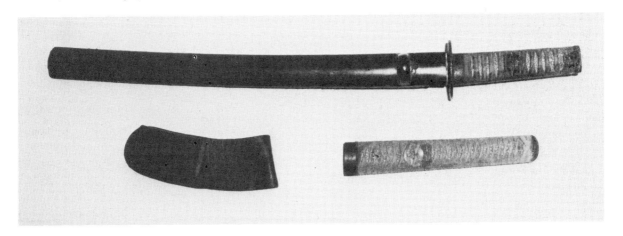

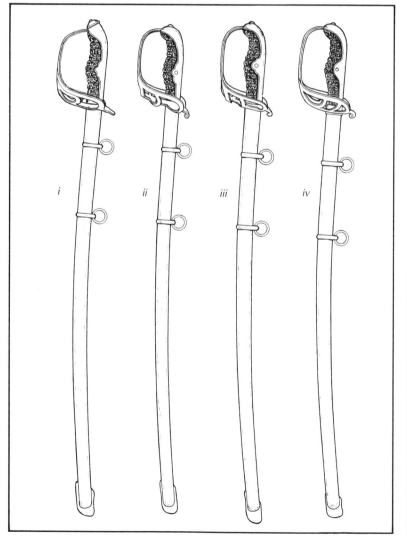

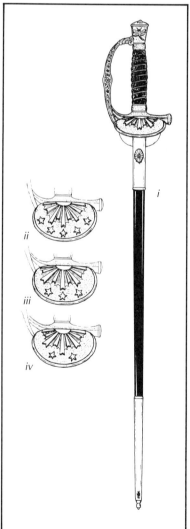

Plate 3. These rebel samurai officers of the Satsuma rebellion (1877) carry their own katanas, rather than the crude rebellion swords that would be carried by other ranks.

Plate 4. A Japanese general in winter uniform at Mukden, Manchuria, in 1905. The sword is indistinct but appears to be the army officers' pattern of c.1871 with a leather combat cover over the scabbard.

Army and airforce swords

Fig. 2. Army sword patterns:-
i) Infantry adjutants and non-commissioned officers' sword c.1877.
ii) Cavalry, artillery, transport and engineers non-commissioned officers' and adjutants' sword, c.1877.
iii) Cavalry, artillery, transport and infantry non-commissioned officers' sword, c.1873.
iv) Army officers' sword, c.1871.

Fig. 3. An army officers' full dress sword pattern, c.1873.
i) The complete sword for company officers (field officers had a decorated chape).
General officers' ranks were indicated on the shellguards:
ii) General.
iii) Lieutenant-general.
iv) Major-general.

They appear to have been carried by other ranks, being found as both katana and wakizashi. Their blades are inferior and rarely signed. Hilt fittings (i.e., tsuba, fuchi and kashira) are plain blackened iron, while the menuki (hilt ornaments) consist of plain iron washers. Occasionally the tsuba may be of a slightly better quality – decorated and even signed – but will still invariably be of blackened iron.

The most noticeable feature is the hilt binding, which is rough braid or canvas wound to give almost triangular openings of exposed samē (rayskin) instead of the traditional diamond shape.

The saya (scabbard) pattern features the traditional black lacquer finish over a wood liner, with projecting kurikata and accessory slot. It is doubtful if kogai and kozuka were ever carried; as may be expected, quality is poor.

The many variations utilise variable-quality fittings and slight differences in hilt-binding technique. As representations of the last samurai battles, however, at least one of these swords deserves a place in every collection.

Fig. 9 i; plates. 2, 3.

ARMY SWORDS: 1871, 1873 AND 1877 PATTERNS

Information on early military swords prior to the introduction of the kyu-guntō pattern around 1900 is scarce and the swords themselves are rarely encountered. Introduction dates are also somewhat tenuous, and many have been accepted by this book on the basis of *Nippon-no-Gunso* by Sasama (Tokyo, 1970).

From 1868 until at least 1871, the traditional katana was worn thrust through the waist sash of a uniform or carried by a frog and shoulder sling or belt.

Fig. 2 illustrates the earliest patterns of prescribed military swords. Unfortunately none has yet been located to confirm the following details, based on contemporary military prints.

The steel scabbards are likely to have been plated, with brass or gilt finished hilt fittings and curved single-edged blades. The grips had wire-bound grooves and were probably wood, shagreen or horn. Totally European in appearance, the swords may only be identifiable as Japanese by arsenal markings – if, indeed, there are any.

Fig. 2; plate 4.

ARMY OFFICERS' DRESS SWORD, ABOUT 1873

1873 appears to be the year officers were authorised a special full-dress sword (fig. 3) based on the European short or court pattern.

The hilt fittings are brass, probably gilded for senior officers. The rear guard folds downwards to lie flat, against the body, while obverse guard decoration displayed the owner's rank by the number of stars. The grip may be either black or white samē (rayskin), leather or possibly horn with gilt-wire bound grooves.

The black leather scabbard has two gilt-brass mounts, the upper having a decorated frog stud for suspension purposes. The only

Plate 5. A variation of the army officers' dress sword pattern of about 1873, with an ancestral blade and a black samē hilt. Suspension is by chain hanger. The purpose of the unusual white cord scabbard binding on this very rare item is unknown. This example appears to have been made for a company officer. (Han Bing Siong collection.)

Plate 6. The hilt of the army officers' dress sword shown in plate 5. (Han Bing Siong collection.)

distinction between field and company officers' swords appears to be the fully engraved scabbard chape of the former. General officers' rank was determined by the number of stars on the obverse guard.

A slim, straight tapering blade is usually encountered but a rare variation with a curved ancestral blade is known. This is fitted with a single suspension mount for use with a sword belt and sling or chain hanger.

Fig. 3; plates 5–8.

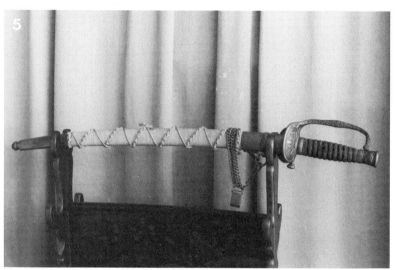

16

Fig. 4. Kyu-guntō sword rank distinctions.
i) General officers' fully decorated backstrap with chrysanthemum (kiku) blossom at the top. Note the silver mon near the base, probably of the Torii family.
ii) Field officers' almost fully decorated backstrap.
iii) Company officers' partly decorated backstrap. Note the engraved mon of the Fukawa family near the base.

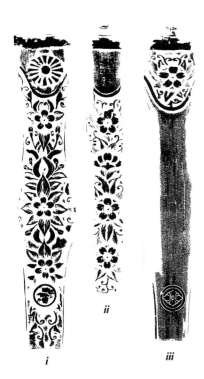

i   *ii*   *iii*

Plate 7. The full dress uniform shown with the army dress sword pattern of *c.*1873.

Plate 8. This first class army surgeon of the Russo-Japanese War (1904–5) carries an army dress sword of the *c.*1873 pattern. Use of the chain hanger indicates the variant with hand-forged blade. The grip is white samē.

ARMY KYU-GUNTO PATTERN

This 'Kyu-guntō', or proto-military sword, must have superseded the 1877 sword patterns shown in fig. 2 with the possible exception of the cavalry type. The introduction date has not been established; one source suggests 1874, which must be regarded as doubtful – otherwise, the kyu-guntō would have *preceded* the 1877 patterns. Dating to the end of the nineteenth century is more likely. The term 'kyu-guntō' should also apply to the earlier patterns but, to comply with the practice of western collectors, it will only be used here for this model and its naval equivalent (qv).

Early examples are thought to have mass-produced blades but most survivors originate from the Russo-Japanese War (1904–5) and usually display hand-forged or ancestral blades. They were carried until superseded by shin-guntō in the early 1930s, though many senior officers continued to carry them during the Second World War.

The hilts are gilt-finished brass with a small pierced obverse guard of sakura (cherry blossom) design and a long, thin knucklebow. The backstrap is wholly or partially engraved according to rank (fig. 4), a general officers' pattern incorporating a kiku or chrysanthemum blossom near the pommel. The grips are rough or polished white samē (rayskin) or, in rare cases, tortoise-shell – normally confined to swords of field and general officers. Black samē is also sometimes found. Gilt-wire binding fills the grip grooves.

Hilts of extreme length can be found when traditional blades are utilised. They are retained by a removable bamboo peg, the mekugi, which passes through the blade tang. Swords with mass-produced blades have shorter hilts that may be removed by unscrewing the pommel-top nut in the same manner as a 'parade sabre'. A few hand-forged blades have been found with tangs tapered and threaded for this kind of fixing.

A decorated press stud with a spring clip, set in the fuchi (collar), engages a slot in the scabbard mouth to retain the sword. Secondary retention by means of a leather strap and press studs is also found (fig. 7).

The metal scabbards are painted or nickel or chromium-plated, and have wood liners. A second (lower) ashi or suspension mount, when present, is normally removable; a slot on the top of the mount slides over the scabbard shoe. Contemporary photographs seem to indicate that the two-ashi style was used with the two-sling full dress sword belt, while the one-ashi fitting was confined to the service belt with its single hanger of chain or leather.

Non-commissioned officers carried a similar sword with plain brass mounts, the backstrap often lacking the side ears. Mass-produced blades and painted metal scabbards are prevalent.

There are many variations of this sword pattern, differing largely in quality of fittings and the amount of decoration (figs 5, 6).

Figs 4-7; plates 9-15.

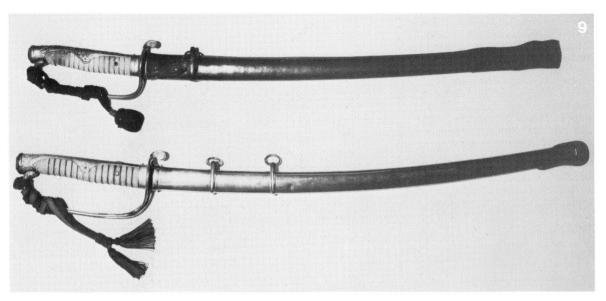

Fig. 5. An unusual partially-decorated general officers' Kyu-guntō backstrap with a chrysanthemum (kiku) motif.

Plate 9. The army company officers' kyu-guntō (bottom) has a two-hanger metal scabbard. The lower mount is removable. The field officers' kyu-guntō (top) has a brown leather combat cover to protect the scabbard. (R. Gregory collection.)

Plate 10. An army kyu-guntō scabbard showing the slot in the lower (removable) suspension mount that allows it to pass over the scabbard shoe. (R. Gregory collection.)

Plate 11. Four kyu-guntō backstraps. *Left to right*: company officer; field officer; general officer; general officer variant, only partially decorated. (R. Gregory collection.)

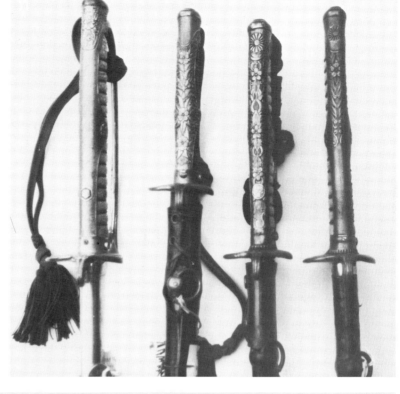

Plate 12. A comparison of kyu-guntō hilt lengths. The upper sword has two suspension mounts, the lower being removable, and an unusual black samé grip. Both are company officers' examples. (R. Gregory collection.)

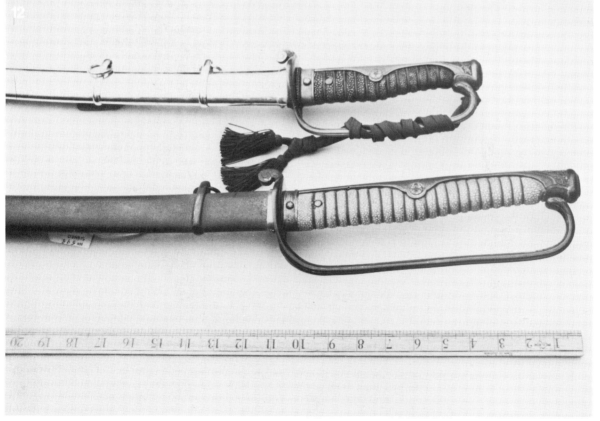

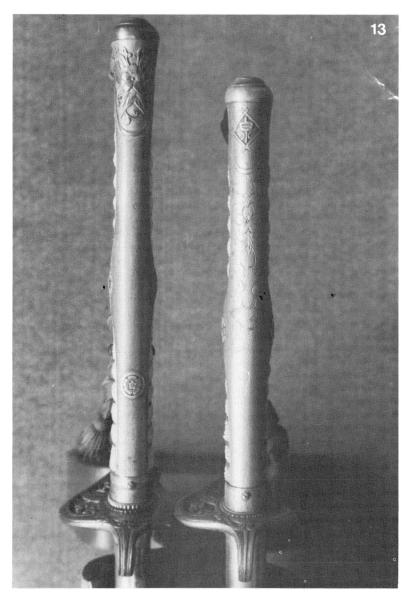

Plate 13. Two army officers' kyu-guntō hilt backstraps. That on the left is the standard company officers' pattern, with a silver mon of the Oda family. That on the right is most unusual; made to special order, it incorporates the character mon of the Izumi family. (Han Bing Siong collection.)

Plate 14. Army Captain Orada, who was responsible for foreign correspondents in the Russo-Japanese War of 1904–5, has his kyu-guntō hooked in the regain position.

Plate 15. A Japanese infantry lieutenant of the Russo-Japanese War period, with a short kyu-guntō.

Fig. 6. A rare and unusual army officers' kyu-guntō backstrap variant with flags, made to special order. The flag design appears to be that of Manchuoko (Manchuria) and may indicate usage by a Manchurian officer serving in the Japanese army.

Fig. 7. Secondary retention by a strap fitted to a kyu-guntō leather combat cover.

ARMY OFFICERS' PARADE SABRE

This light duty sword, similar to the kyu-guntō, was carried by officers of all ranks. Probably introduced with (or just after) the kyu-guntō, it must have superseded the dress sword of 1873.

The curved, plated, mass-produced blade — fullered on both sides — is quite flexible, but blunt and useless as a fighting weapon. A commonly encountered fake acid-etched yakiba (tempered edge) was an extra-cost option. The hilt design copies the kyu-guntō even to the extent of rank distinction by backstrap engraving. Wire-bound horn grips are normally encountered.

The blade is retained in the scabbard by push fit, although a habaki or blade collar is normally absent. The hilt can be dismantled by removing the decorated pommel nut, the blade tang being threaded at the top.

These swords are common, being carried in the 1930s and almost certainly much later as there was no dress version of the shin-guntō.

Army parade sabres are often wrongly described as police sabres. The latter are clearly distinguishable by the police badge on the hilt (fig. 30).

Figs 4, 30; plates 16-19, 87-8.

CAVALRY TROOPERS' SWORD, ABOUT 1886

The 1877 pattern (fig. 2) appears to have lasted until about 1886. The new troopers' pattern has a plain, black finished steel D-guard, with an eared backstrap and a contoured wooden grip that can be plain or chequered to match the backstrap. The Koishikawa (Tōkyō) or Kokura arsenal mark (fig. 35 i) is often stamped underneath the guard.

The small hole in the guard receives a leather finger loop, which is usually missing.

The mass-produced blades are slightly curved with a wide fuller. Western-style assembly, or accountability, numbers are stamped on the ricasso and also on the scabbard drag. They should match.

The blackened-steel scabbards feature one ashi (suspension mount) and a brass throat.

The blade is fixed to the hilt by a screw through the centre of the grip. The screw head — unique among Japanese swords — has two small holes instead of a slot, and requires a special dismantling tool. The pommel is secured in a similar fashion.

A steel spring clip, fixed to the hilt by the central grip screw, passes through the guard to engage with a raised scabbard throat-fitting on the obverse side.

Although relatively scarce, this sword is not sought after because of its utilitarian, non-Japanese appearance.

Plates 20-5.

Plate 16. Comparative lengths of army officers' parade sabres. The similarity to the full-size kyu-guntō is apparent. (R. Gregory collection.)

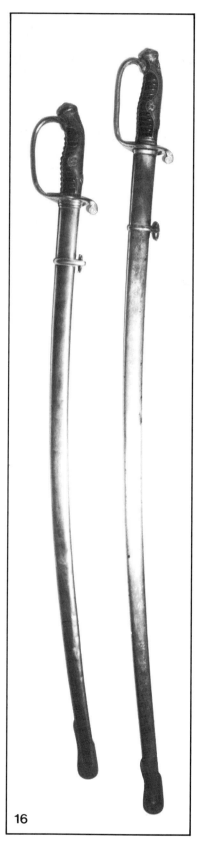

16

Plate 17. Emperor Hirohito with an army parade sabre, c.1936.

Plate 18. Prince Chichibu – brother of Emperor Hirohito – at Aldershot, England, in 1937. He has a parade sabre in the regain position. (Courtesy of Han Bing Siong.)

Plate 19. General Sadao Araki displays his scarce two-hanger parade sabre. He was minister of war from 1931 to 1934 and retired in 1936. In 1948, he was sentenced to life imprisonment as a Class A war criminal. (Courtesy of Han Bing Siong.)

Plate 20. This cavalry troopers' sword of the c.1886 pattern has a machine-made blade, blackened steel mounts and a blackened scabbard. The tassel is a shin-guntō pattern dating from the Second World War. (R. Fuller collection.)

NOTE. A variation (or copy?) of this sword appeared on the market in 1985 in large numbers; together with other surrendered Japanese equipment obtained from China, they are reputedly cavalry or police sabres taken in 1945. However, because of their generally excellent condition and certain deviations in materials and design, usage and origin must be accepted with caution. They may be of indigenous manufacture for use in the postwar Chinese armed forces.

The aluminium hilt has a flattened pommel and green plastic grip, both being chequered. The side-mounted spring clip retention system differs slightly from normal. No Japanese arsenal marks are present. The plated blade – indicative of dress use – displays western-style issue or accountability numbers on the ricasso, matching those on the scabbard shoe. These, however, are lightly engraved and not stamped. The steel scabbard has two suspension bands, each fitted with a D-ring. The scabbard and hilt are both painted green, but the general construction does not appear to be Japanese.

No examples from other wartime theatres have yet been reported or examined.

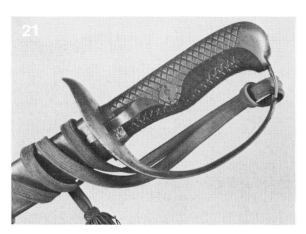

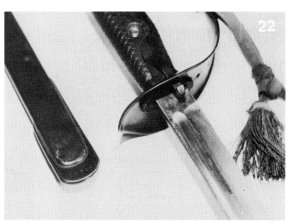

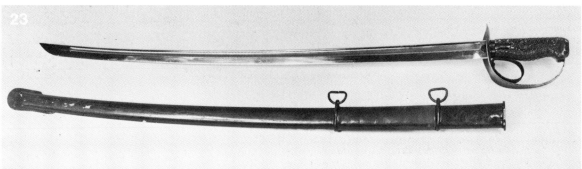

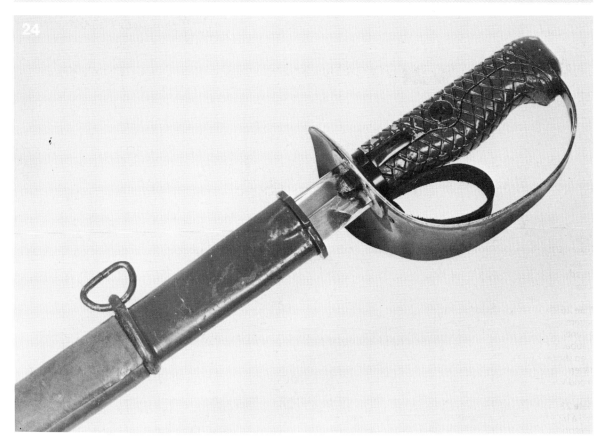

Plate 21. Hilt detail of a cavalry troopers' sword, post-1886. (C. Halvorson collection.)

Plate 22. The cavalry troopers' sword (see plate 20) showing matching assembly or issue numbers, 14790, on the scabbard drag and blade ricasso. (R. Fuller collection.)

Plate 23. A variation or copy of the cavalry troopers' sword pattern of *c*.1886. The aluminium hilt and plastic grip have a green painted finish, and the blade is plated. This sword may have been made after the war for the Chinese armed forces. (R. Fuller collection.)

Plate 24. The aluminium hilt and plastic grip of the sword shown in Plate 23. It is apparent that the push-button spring clip retention differs from that of the cavalry sabre of *c*.1886. (R. Fuller collection.)

Plate 25. A Japanese cavalry trooper in the Russo-Japanese War (1904–5) with the sword pattern of *c*.1886. The buckle on the adjustable sword sling can also be seen.

Plate 26. The cavalry officers' sword pattern of *c*.1886, with gilded brass hilt mounts, a white samē grip and a steel scabbard. The hand-forged blade has been shortened. Note the shin-guntō pattern tassel dating from the Second World War. (R. Gregory collection.)

Plate 27. A cavalry officers' sword hilt, and a backstrap with a silver mon. (R. Gregory collection.)

CAVALRY OFFICERS' SWORD

As may be expected, cavalry officers carried a much more elaborate sword than the troopers. Mass-produced or ancestral blades are used. Though the introduction date has not been determined, this rare sword may be contemporaneous with the troopers' pattern or perhaps the kyu-guntō – about 1886.

A gilt finished D-guard, similar to the troopers' pattern, is distinguished by a series of slots and an engraved backstrap (fig. 8). It is doubtful if a rank system of decoration was used, as only one design has yet been encountered.

The wire-bound grip of white samē or horn is similar to the kyu-guntō type. It also incorporates a press-stud spring clip retention system.

The nickel or chromium-plated scabbards have a shoe and one ashi (suspension mount).

The small number of independent cavalry units retained until 1945 may have carried both troopers' and officers' swords. Lieutenant-General Masao Baba, commander of the 37th Army in Borneo, surrendered such a sword at Labuan, South Borneo, in 1945. Now in the Australian War Memorial Museum, Canberra, (item no. AWM 31262), it has a very long hilt fitted with a blade by Kanenobu of Mino, c.1650.

Fig. 8; plates 26, 27.

ARMY OFFICERS' SHIN-GUNTŌ PATTERN

Japanese military involvement in Manchuria and China in the early 1930s generated strong nationalistic feelings that were reflected in the shin-guntō (neo-army sword) introduced in 1933–4 to replace the kyu-guntō. Based on the traditional tachi, the slung sword, the shin-guntō is the most common of all Japanese military swords and was carried throughout the Second World War as a weapon.

The tsuka (hilt) consists of tape – usually brown, but sometimes green, blue or black bound over white samē (rayskin) on a wooden base. Hilt fittings consist of matching brass kabuto-gane (pommel) and fuchi (collar) decorated with sakura (cherryblossom). The hilt ornaments are in the form of three sakura. A brass guard, the tsuba, is cast in aoi shape and decorated with four raised sakura on each side. The guard may be solid or pierced, the latter rumoured to have been initially restricted to senior officers. Seppa, totalling four to eight, lie on each side of the tsuba, being called dai-seppa, ko-seppa and seppa in descending order of size. The dai-seppa is copper; the ko-seppa, shakudo or gilt; and the seppa, brass, silver-plated or aluminium. The hilt can be dismantled by removing a bamboo peg (mekugi) that passes through the tang.

Rank is determined by tassel colouring (see Chapter 7). The tassel is tied around a plain or decorated brass or copper loop (saru-te) fixed to the kabuto-gane.

The steel or alloy scabbards have wood liners and four fittings, comprising kuchi-gane (throat), ashi (suspension mount), shibabiki

Fig. 8. Details of a post-1904 cavalry officers' sword hilt.
Top: the backstrap decoration with a silver butterfly mon of the Ikeda family.
Bottom: a plan of obverse guard showing the cut-out pattern.

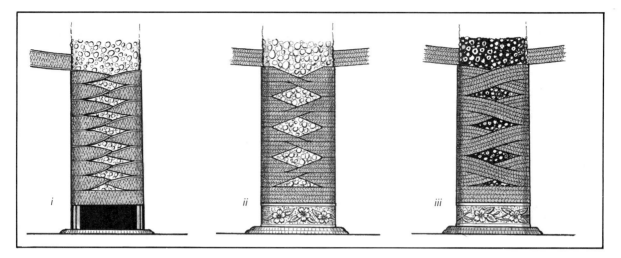

Fig. 9. Three common variations of hilt binding styles.
i) Rebellion sword.
ii) Shin- and kai-guntō swords.
iii) Kai-guntō sword.

Fig. 10. The suspension mounts (ashi) found on metal and lacquered scabbards.
i) Shin-guntō for army officers (brass, copper or plated steel).
ii) Kai-guntō for naval officers (brass or copper).
iii) Shin-guntō for army officers, late-1944 pattern (iron).

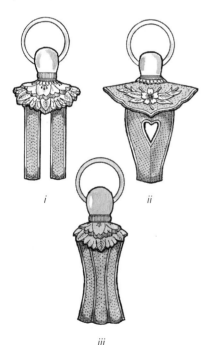

(strengthening band) and ishizuke (drag). They are painted green, brown or khaki. Black is said to have been used only from 1943 onwards. Known variations include rough brown lacquer over a canvas base and brown-lacquered shagreen. Polished samē is another rare variant. The fittings are decorated to match the hilt and are quite distinct from the naval kai-guntō (fig. 10).

On rare occasions, a second (lower) ashi may be found. Unlike the upper one, this may be removed without the taking off the lower two scabbard fittings. Figs 11 and 12 show four variations. They are thought to have been used only by senior officer who retained kyu-guntō full dress belts, which had two slings. An army general was photographed in 1935 with such a sword. However, two photographs taken at Shanghai in 1937 show naval officers in land-warfare uniforms with two-hanger army shin-guntō that may indicate the 'mixed function' of this service. These officers would normally have carried the kai-guntō.

A brown leather cover, shrunk and stitched over a wooden liner, is very common and termed a 'field scabbard'. Ashi patterns for these vary (fig. 13), but differ from the metal scabbard version. Metal or lacquered scabbards may be protected by a removable leather 'combat cover'.

The blades of these swords are either machine-made, modern hand-forged gendaitō or ancestral, and are all found with a habaki (blade collar).

A push-button spring clip retains the swords in metal scabbards, as found on kyu-guntō, while a press-studded leather strap going through the tsuba sufficed for field scabbards.

Apart from the tsuba and seppa, all metal fittings have a tarnish-resistant matt brown finish with edges highlighted in gilt. This brown finish should not be polished off intentionally in favour of the brass beneath.

Many variations are encountered, including part-military and part-civilian. One variant has a standard army hilt and metal scabbard fittings. Its scabbard, however, is black lacquer on a wooden base – not normally found with shin-guntō unless an old civilian scabbard has been utilised. Black samē or canvas appears under the hilt binding and the blade tang bears an anchor-in-circle stamp (fig. 35 xxi), inferring that it was carried by an army officer with naval connections or vice versa. Alternatively, it may have been assembled from mixed army and navy components when the demand for kai-guntō dropped. Examples examined all appeared to be new or in excellent condition, so the possibility exists that they are postwar assemblies.

At the time of writing, spurious officers' shin-guntō are appearing on the market from Spain and Pakistan. The former is complete with facsimile tang signatures while the latter has badly cast standard-pattern hilt fittings, poor-quality hilt binding and a crude blade.

Figs 1, 9-20, 35; plates 28-48.

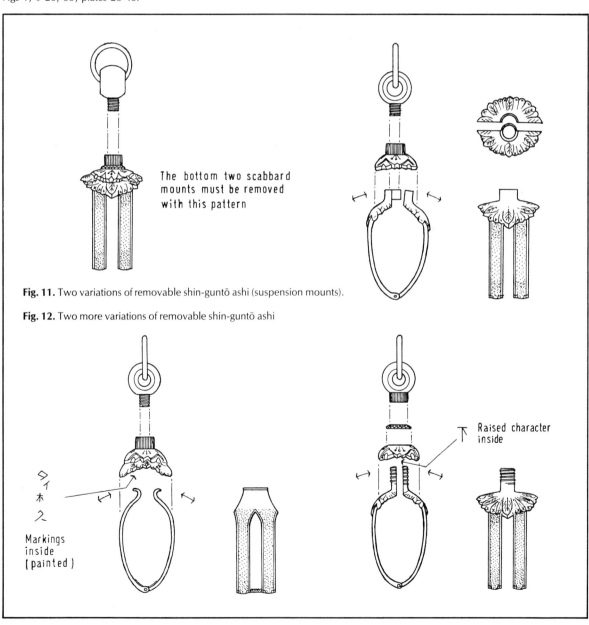

Fig. 11. Two variations of removable shin-guntō ashi (suspension mounts).

Fig. 12. Two more variations of removable shin-guntō ashi

The bottom two scabbard mounts must be removed with this pattern

Raised character inside

Markings inside (painted)

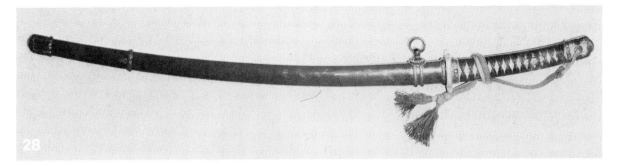

Plate 29. A collection of military tsuba (guard) and seppa (packing pieces). *Top to bottom*:
i) The army NCOs' brass shin-guntō, regular pattern.
ii) Pierced shin-guntō tsuba for spring clip retention.
iii) A solid shin-guntō tsuba for spring clip retention (left), or leather strap retention (right).
iv) A naval kai-guntō tsuba with dai-seppa of alternating rays of brass and copper.
(R. Gregory collection.)

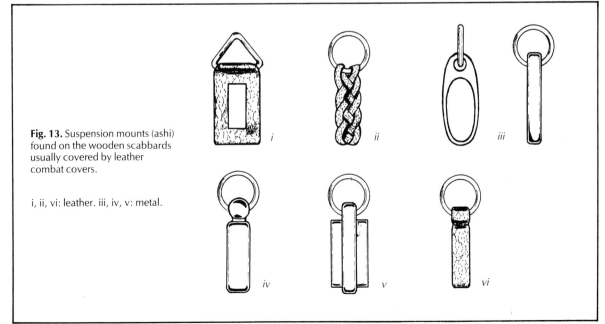

Fig. 13. Suspension mounts (ashi) found on the wooden scabbards usually covered by leather combat covers.

i, ii, vi: leather. iii, iv, v: metal.

Fig. 14. Hilt fittings – typical assembly and 'arsenal' stamps.
i-iii) Shin-guntō dai-seppa: assembly numbers 40, 28 and 880 (accompanied by mark ⌇ [ma]) respectively.
iv) Shin-guntō tsuba with an unidentified arsenal or acceptance stamp.
v) The obverse and reverse of a kai-guntō seppa with unusual stamps of an anchor within a cherryblossom (Toyokawa naval arsenal) and roman lettering T.E.C. (significance unknown).

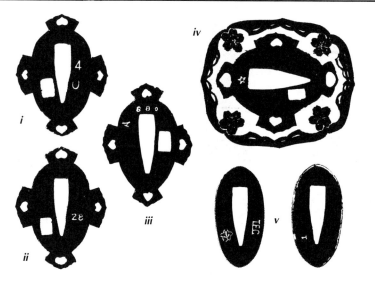

i

ii

iii

iv

v

Fig. 15. A rare pattern of officers' shin-guntō ishizuke (chape), with a drag. A kai-guntō version is also found with identical markings. Probably patent marks.

REVERSE

OBVERSE

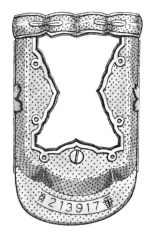

30

Plate 31. General Tomoyuki Yamashita, the 'Tiger of Malaya'. His shin-guntō has a general officers' tassel. (Private photograph collection.)

Plate 32. Shin-guntō of General Tomoyuki Yamashita, conqueror of Malaya and 14th Area Army Commander during the defence of the Philippines. Note the general officers' tassel (brown and red, with yellow zig-zag stitches and yellow tassel). The blade is signed FUJIWARA KANENAGA, possibly of Sagami province c.1640–80. (West Point Military Academy Museum.)

Plate 33. An army officers' shin-guntō with a scarce brown-lacquered samē-covered scabbard. The rayskin (samē) nodules show through as white spots. This type is usually associated with naval swords. (R. Gregory collection.)

Plate 30. Various metal tassel loops (saru-te) from officers' shin-guntō hilts. (R. Gregory collection.)

32   33

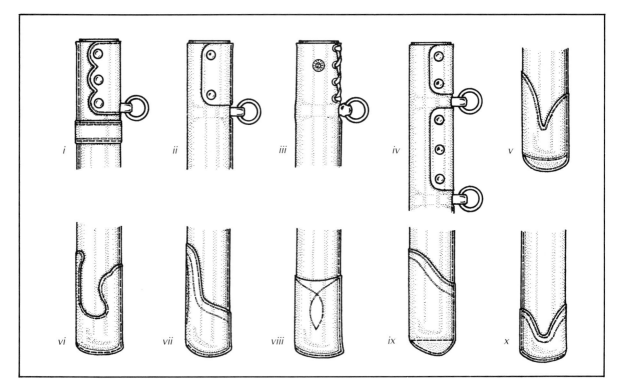

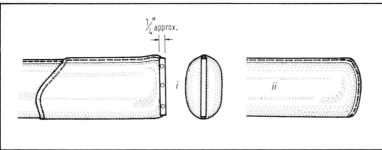

Fig. 16. Leather scabbard details:
i-iii) Typical army throat fastenings.
iv) A naval throat fastening for a two hanger sword.
v-x) Typical thickened chapes found on all field scabbards.

Fig. 17. Unusual leather field scabbard chape details.
i) A brass or copper reinforcement piece.
ii) A single-thickness plain leather cover over a wooden liner.

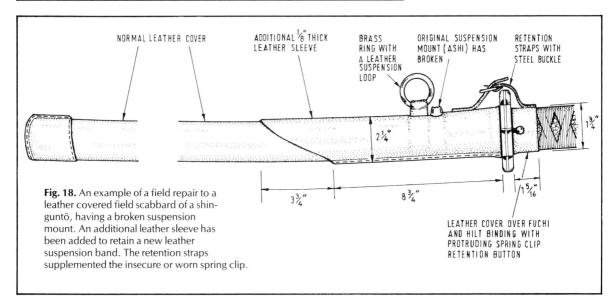

NORMAL LEATHER COVER

ADDITIONAL 1/8" THICK LEATHER SLEEVE

BRASS RING WITH A LEATHER SUSPENSION LOOP

ORIGINAL SUSPENSION MOUNT (ASHI) HAS BROKEN

RETENTION STRAPS WITH STEEL BUCKLE

LEATHER COVER OVER FUCHI AND HILT BINDING WITH PROTRUDING SPRING CLIP RETENTION BUTTON

Fig. 18. An example of a field repair to a leather covered field scabbard of a shin-guntō, having a broken suspension mount. An additional leather sleeve has been added to retain a new leather suspension band. The retention straps supplemented the insecure or worn spring clip.

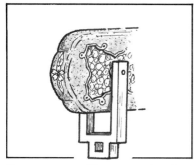

Fig. 19. An unusual brass saru-te found on an army officer's shin-guntō; probably a field-made replacement.

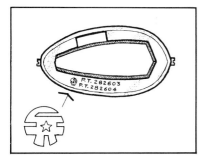

Fig. 20. These rare markings on a standard regulation shin-guntō metal scabbard-throat (kuchi-gane) are probably patent stamps, which may indicate a prototype or manufacturing date soon after the introduction of this sword type.

Plate 34. This army officers' shin-guntō has a rare type of field scabbard fitted with an additional suspension ring at the bottom. Thus the sword can be slung across the back on a leather or cloth sling in rough terrain, leaving both hands free. (R. Gregory collection.)

Plate 35. A shin-guntō with a green canvas foul-weather scabbard cover having a leather chape. These covers are often tied around the middle for extra security. (R. Gregory collection.)

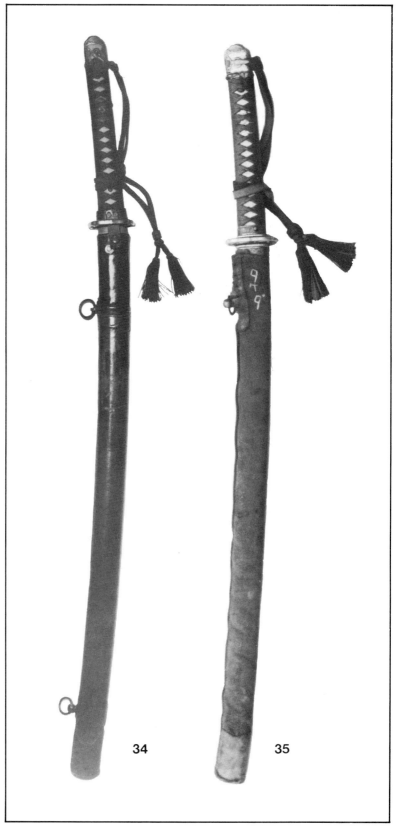

34   35

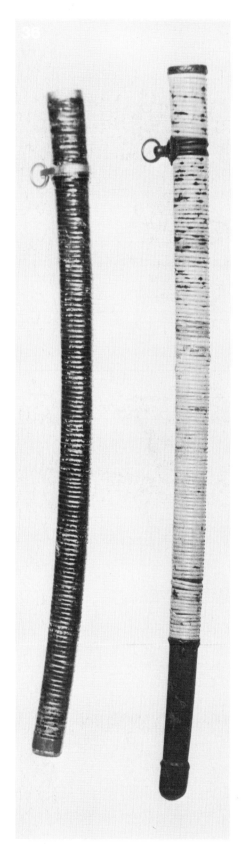

Plate 36. Two unusual shin-guntō scabbard variations. The wooden field scabbard (left) is bound with black lacquered cane. The standard metal scabbard (right) is bound with white cane, perhaps instead of a leather combat cover. (Fuller and Gregory collections.)

Plate 37. An army officers' shin-guntō with a leather-covered civilian katana scabbard. Unusually, two suspension rings are fitted into one suspension mount, but the reason for this is unknown. (R. Fuller collection).

Plate 38. The field scabbard of this shin-guntō incorporates an unusual elongated spring clip and a hinged suspension mount. (R. Gregory collection.)

Plate 39. This is the scarce two-ashi (suspension mount) army officers' shin-guntō. The lower mount unscrews for removal without needing to detach the two bottom scabbard fittings. The scabbard on the left has been fitted with a brown leather combat cover. (R. Gregory collection.)

Plate 40. *Top*: The scarce two-ashi shin-guntō with lower mount detached. *Bottom*: A shira-saya (wooden keeper scabbard for an unmounted blade), converted for military use by the addition of a leather cover, a brass throat and, unusually, two fixed ashi. (R. Fuller collection.)

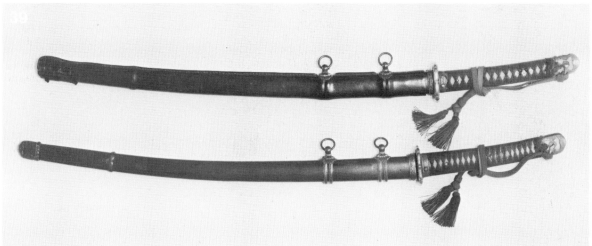

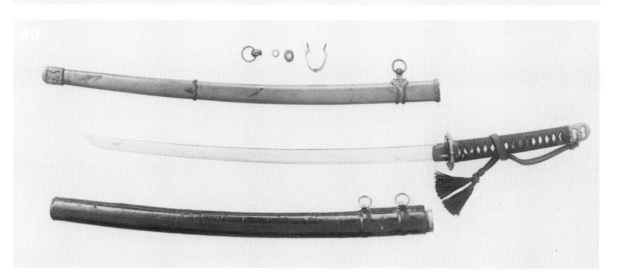

42

41

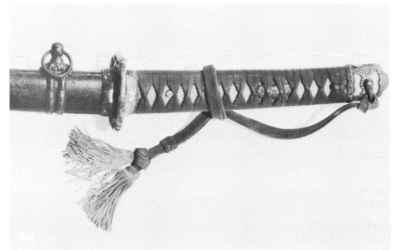

Plate 41. Emperor Hirohito and senior officers on parade in 1936, with two-hanger army shin-guntō. Note that suspension appears to be by one hanger with a short strap connecting the two suspension mounts. This seems to serve no useful purpose.

Plate 42. The outside of a wooden scabbard liner from a shin-guntō metal scabbard. The left centre markings read, in part, 'Respectfully made by the Hatori Sword Shop, Kanda (Tōkyō)'. Why it should be so profusely inscribed is unknown, as it is so unlikely to be seen. (R. Gregory collection.)

Plate 43. Two shin-guntō with scarce scabbard seals formed by a seppa with outer rim projecting downward. The 3mm projection (left) partly covers the scabbard throat (kuchi-ganē), which is recessed to receive it. The 6mm projection (right) covers the throat entirely. (R. Gregory collection.)

Plate 44. An army officers' shin-guntō with a rare sword-retention clip, which also acts as an integral scabbard-mouth cover. See plates 45-7. (R. Gregory collection.)

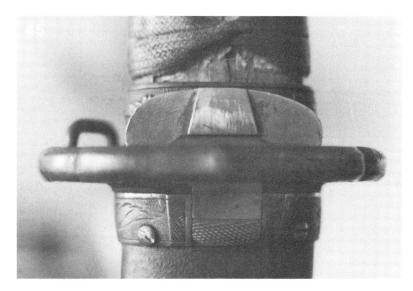

Plates 45-7. A rare pattern of shin-guntō sword-retention clip with an integral scabbard-mouth cover. (Han Bing Siong collection.)

Plate 45. The cover through the tsuba acts as clip to hold the sword.

Plate 46. The scabbard mouth with the cover closed.

Plate 47. The underside of the tsuba showing the slot through which the cover passes to hold the sword.

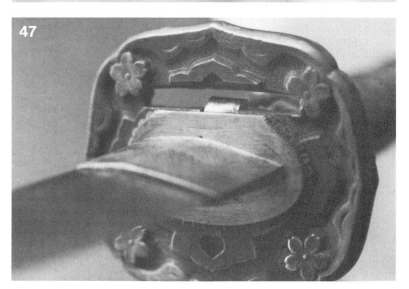

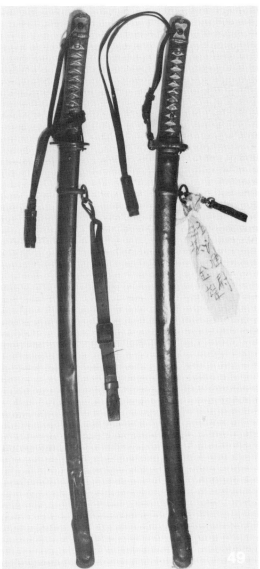

Plate 48. An army officer bowing at a surrender ceremony in Saigon, 26 November 1945. His tasselled shin-guntō is in the regain position. (IWM photograph SE 5689).

Plate 49. Two army NCOs' shin-guntō with cast aluminium hilts painted to resemble the officers' tape-bound pattern. The swords have plain blackened iron tsuba (left) and brass aoi-shaped tsuba (right). The brown leather knots have either a continuous strap or one broken by a buckle near the end. The latter is only found on swords with brass tsuba, for fixing as shown. Use of a brown leather combat cover is indicative of a senior NCO. The linen surrender or transportation tag reads 'Hori Kaeo, Jun-i [Warrant Officer]'. The suspension straps are brown leather. (R. Gregory collection.)

ARMY NON-COMMISSIONED OFFICERS' SHIN-GUNTŌ PATTERN

This totally mass-produced copy of the officers' shin-guntō was introduced, it is thought, in 1933 or 1934 and issued to NCOs as a regulation requirement.

The most distinctive feature is the hilt, which is a complete cast aluminium (sometimes brass) copy of the officers' pattern. Well detailed, it is painted to represent the normal coloured binding and samē. The separate plain copper fuchi bears the Koishikawa Kokura arsenal symbol (fig. 35 i). Brass aoi-shape or, occasionally thin blackened-iron tsuba are used with only two seppa. The hilt is retained by two dome-headed screws.

The painted olive green steel scabbards have one ashi and a fixed shoe. A spring clip, affixed to the top edge of the hilt, passes through the tsuba to engage with a throat fitting and retain the sword in the scabbard. Leather combat covers are rarely fitted, but may denote usage by a senior NCO or warrant officer when found.

The mass-produced blade, fullered on both sides, is stamped with arabic (western-style) assembly or accountability numbers which match those stamped on the brass scabbard throat (fig. 21).

It is rumoured that these swords were made in England or Germany to the order of the Japanese government, but this has not been substantiated and seems most unlikely.

An emergency-issue variation was made in the field, the entire hilt – including fuchi – being a single crude aluminium casting. A thin oval blackened-iron tsuba is accompanied by two copper seppa. The hilt is held by a removable wooden peg (mekugi) to a poor-quality forged blade made from one piece of steel. An inferior black lacquered scabbard has a brown leather combat cover, possibly glued on.

Mint examples of the normal regulation army NCO shin-guntō pattern are currently appearing on the market. Complete in every detail, they are reportedly made in India or Pakistan to deceive the collector.

Figs 21, 35; plates 49-52.

Plate 50. The matching assembly or accountability numbers 38254 on the blade and scabbard throat of an army NCOs' shin-guntō. The Koishikawa arsenal symbol is discernible on the far left. (R. Fuller collection).

Fig. 21. Details of NCOs' shin-gunto blade and fuchi markings. Note the right-hand symbol of four cannonballs (ii and iii), which was shared by Koishikawa and Kokura Arsenals in 1929–35. The centre control stamp, however, was only used by Koishikawa Arsenal prior to 1936.
i) Typical sword-blade markings. Note the Koishikawa Arsenal control stamp (pre-1936).
ii) Markings on the fuchi of the above sword.
iii) Markings on another fuchi.

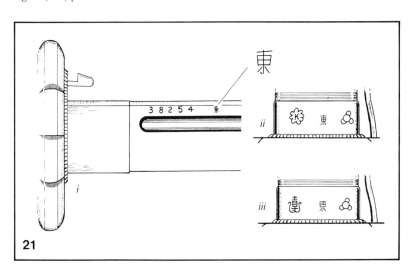

21

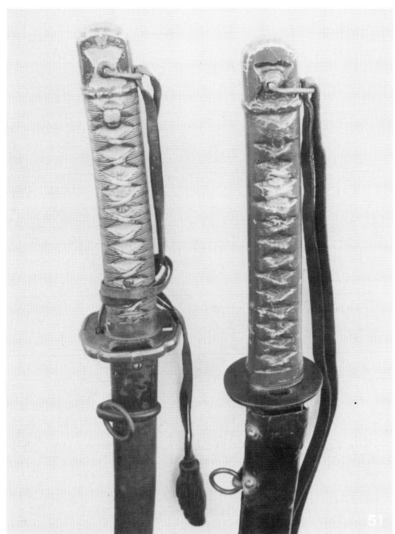

Plate 51. NCOs' shin-guntō hilts.
Left: the regular aluminium pattern, cast and painted to resemble the officers' pattern. The fine detailing is apparent. Brass tsuba.
Right: the crudely cast aluminium emergency pattern, with blackened steel tsuba. (R. Fuller collection.)

Plate 52. The very rare removable brown leather sleeve for conversion of the single-hanger NCOs' shin-guntō scabbard to two. It may have been used by a warrant officer serving in China, where this item was apparently obtained. (R. Fuller collection.)

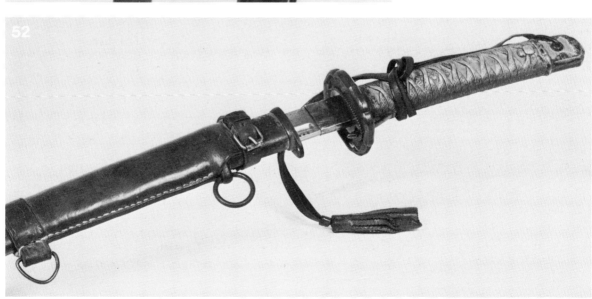

AIRFORCE AND AIRBORNE UNIT SWORDS

Photographs contemporaneous with the war period show aircrew carrying standard shin-guntō. They were even carried in the cockpit or clipped into an access panel in the fuselage.

A very rare miniature shin-guntō is known to exist but details are unobtainable. It appears to be no more than 18in long and complete in every detail down to the green-painted metal scabbard. Said to be for use by the airforce, it is doubtful that it encountered much favour.

A standard shin-guntō with a leather-covered field scabbard has been found with original embossed parachutist wings on the cover obverse (fig. 23). The specially made brass saru-te (tassel loop) bears the Japanese pilot's badge design. Such personalisation was presumably offered by the sword retailer at extra cost. This rare sword must have been used by an airborne-unit officer.

Figs 22, 23.

ARMY OFFICERS' PATTERN SHIN-GUNTŌ, LATE 1944

Towards the end of 1944, according to *Nippon-no-Gunso* by Sasama, the standard shin-guntō was superseded by a new ersatz pattern designed to conserve brass – an essential war material. Often referred to as the naval landing forces (marines) or kempeitai (military police) officers' sword, no evidence supports sole usage by either group.

The hilt and scabbard mounts are blackened iron, the sakura motif being restricted to the fuchi (collar), ashi (suspension mount) and ishizuke (chape). The standard menuki 'hilt ornaments', are made of blackened iron. A plain oval blackened-iron tsuba is standard, although an openwork design was apparently originally envisaged. None of the latter has been found. The hilt is retained by two dome-headed screws that pass through the blade tang, the heads being on opposite sides.

The scabbards have three fittings, the shibabiki being abandoned. Some may be metal, painted light khaki, while others are rough brown or black lacquer over a wooden base.

The most distinctive feature is the close-bound 'battle type' (Katatemaki) braid hilt, which may be green, brown or orange-red, often heavily lacquered. Artificial samē is commonly used.

Retention is usually by the normal push button and spring clip. Two push buttons are sometimes found, one set in the fuchi and the other in the kuchi-gane (scabbard throat).

The blade types parallel those of the shin-guntō but, if dated, normally range from 1943 to as late as June 1945. The widely spaced peg holes help to identify blades with these mounts.

No saru-tē (tassel loop) was used, the plain brown tassel being looped through a large hole in the kabuto-gane (pommel cap) and stitched underneath (fig. 41 iii). Field uniforms lacked identifying rank badges by this time and the coloured system of tassels may have been abandoned for safety.

Figs 10, 41; plates 53-6.

Fig. 22. A very rare miniature shin-guntō, reputed to have been carried by airforce officers.

Fig. 23. These rare markings on a shin-guntō indicate use by airborne or airforce officers.
i) Embossed on a leather field scabbard.
ii) A raised design on a specially-made brass saru-te (knot loop).

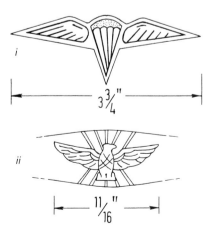

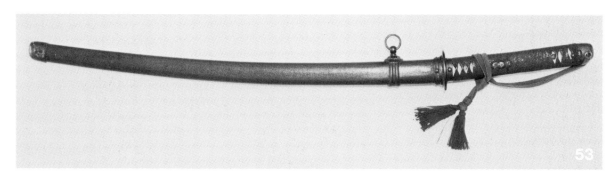

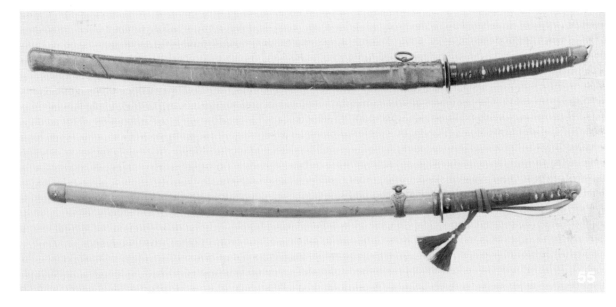

Plate 53. A late-1944 pattern army officers' shin-guntō with blackened iron mounts and a plain brown tassel. This example has a rough textured brown-lacquered scabbard. (R. Gregory collection).

Plate 54. The hilt of the late-1944 pattern army officers' shin-guntō (see plate 53) with lacquered hilt binding. Note the two press studs on the hilt collar (fuchi) and the scabbard throat (kuchi-ganē). (R. Gregory collection).

Plate 55. *Top*: An 'ersatz' sword, probably made in an occupied area such as Java.
Bottom: a late-1944 pattern shin-guntō with a metal scabbard. (R. Fuller collection.)

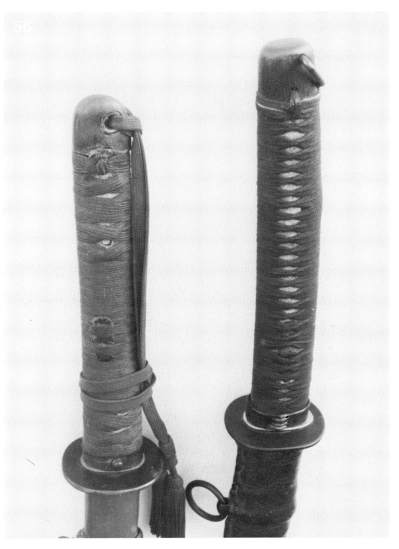

Plate 56. *Left*: a late-1944 patten shin-guntō with unlacquered green tape binding.
Right: an ersatz sword with red tape binding. (R. Fuller collection.)

Plate 57. An ancestral samurai short-sword (wakizashi) and dirk (tantō) mounted for military use with a protective brown leather combat cover, a foul weather hilt cover, and a retention and suspension mount dating from the Second World War. It is rare to find a tantō that has seen military use. (R. Gregory collection.)

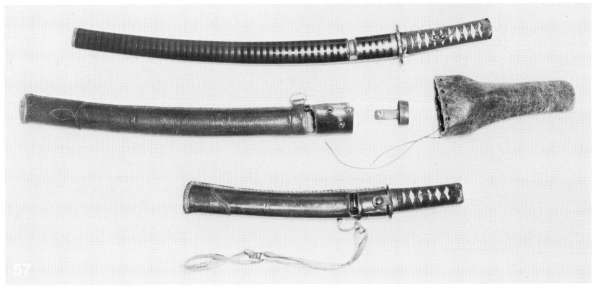

ARMY SHIN-GUNTŌ HOME DEFENCE PATTERN

A variation of the late 1944 shin-guntō exists, 'liberated' from a pile of swords scheduled for destruction in Japan. It is one of a number reputed to have been made for the home defence of Japan when the expected American invasion occurred (fig. 24).

Obviously an ersatz type, its mounts are a combination of black-painted steel or brass with a gunmetal finish. They are also of a distinctive pattern. An inferior quality braid, dyed brown, is bound over a yellowish-white canvas in the same manner as the 1944 pattern. Identical menuki are fitted.

An unsigned blade fits into a brown gunmetal-finish steel scabbard. Once again, the sword is held in the scabbard by a push button spring clip. The appropriate type of tassel is unknown.

Fig. 24.

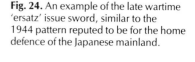

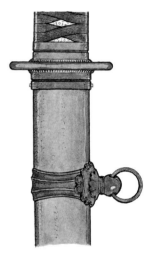

Fig. 24. An example of the late wartime 'ersatz' issue sword, similar to the 1944 pattern reputed to be for the home defence of the Japanese mainland.

SHŌWA PERIOD CIVILIAN SWORDS

Civilian wakizashi and katana dating earlier than the Meiji period are often found wholly or partially adapted for military use in the Second World War. Shōwa period civilian-style katana, which appear to be older samurai swords to the untutored eye, are not so common.

A strong revival of sword and blade collecting occurred during the war years, when those who could not afford ancestral blades bought new examples.

A number of Shōwa-period katana has been examined with mass-produced fittings in which the fuchi, kashira and tsuba are generally decorated to match one another. The garnitures include:

i) raised sakura (cherryblossom) in brass;
ii) raised bamboo leaves in brass, with a browned finish or sometimes grey-silver plated;
iii) raised sea shells and starfish in blackened steel, the tsuba sometimes differing (e.g., birds flying over water).

Menuki designs vary and hilt binding is normally either black or blue-green. The blades are usually modern hand-forged gendaitō. Civilian-style lacquered scabbards of different colours are used, though a brown leather combat cover may be fitted for military use. The kurikata is present, but slots for accessories are normally omitted.

Plates 57-64.

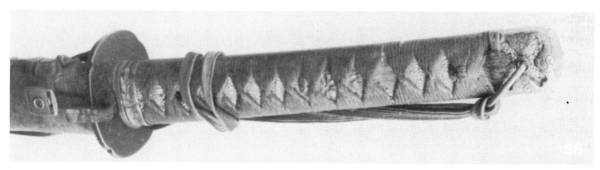

Plate 59. This Shōwa period traditional civilian sword (katana) has mass-produced fittings and a brown lacquered scabbard. Note the rare plain gold label on the scabbard which may be the manufacturer's or retailer's trademark. (R. Fuller collection.)

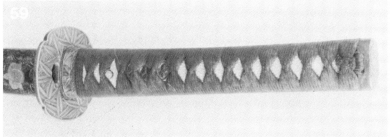

Plate 60. This Shōwa-period civilian katana hilt has a blackened iron tsuba engraved with sakura (cherryblossom). The leather collar and the retaining strap passing through the tsuba is clearly visible. (R. Gregory collection.)

Plate 61. Another view of the Shōwa-period civilian katana shown in Plate 60. Note the braiding saru-te (knot loop) through the kashira (pommel) and the leather suspension band looped through the brown leather combat cover. (R. Gregory collection.)

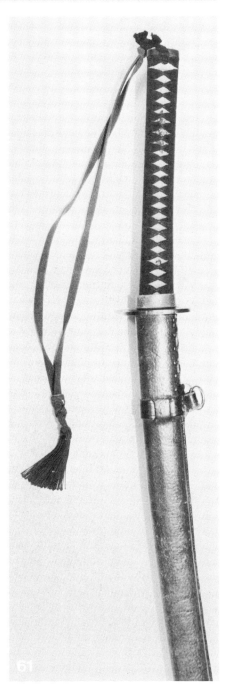

Plate 58. A poor quality shin-guntō with civilian brass mounts and an iron tsuba, bound for military use and featuring standard army-pattern menuki (hilt ornaments). (R. Fuller collection.)

昭和十五年十月八日

左近允尚正

Plate 63. Shōwa-period tsuba (guards) and fuchi (hilt collars) for civilian-mounted swords (katana). (R. Gregory collection.)

Plate 64. This Japanese corporal holds a civilian katana, which has an officers' tassel fixed to the hilt as shown in fig. 41 ii. As other ranks were not entitled such swords, he probably borrowed it just for the photograph. (Private photograph collection.)

Plate 62. This photograph of Captain (later Vice Admiral) Naomasa Sakonju IJN is signed and dated 8 October 1940. At this time he was commanding officer at Hankow, China, and presented this photograph to Mr Robert Jarvis of the US Consulate. His civilian katana is carried in a leather-covered scabbard, probably fitted with two suspension mounts for naval use. (M. Davis photograph collection.)

LEATHER COVERED SWORDS

These late war or emergency swords are often found with hilts and scabbards entirely covered with leather, except – perhaps – for the kabuto-gane (pommel). The brown leather covering is normally shrunk and stitched to a wooden base on these poor quality items, though hilt covers can be cross-laced through metal eyelets. Retention relies on a leather strap and press stud.

Variations may be encountered without tsuba or kabuto-gane. Even shira-saya (the wooden scabbard used for protecting an unmounted blade) may be covered in leather, although not intended for the poor-quality blades invariably encountered.

Plates 63, 65-7.

EMERGENCY-ISSUE SWORDS

These were made entirely in occupied countries when supplies from Japan ceased. In fact, many were never intended to be carried but were made by off-duty soldiers and guards whose ambition was to own a sword but were forbidden by rank to wear them. Made from scrap steel, they were tested on banana trees – as witnessed by an English POW at Macassar in the Celebes. Possibly some were carried by non-Japanese, such as the Manchurians, Koreans or Formosans conscripted into the Japanese army. They must not be confused with emergency patterns that received official approval.

Variations are numerous. Most have a split-cane or rattan wrapped hilt with no provision for a tassel or knot, and a scabbard with plain iron fittings. The blades are extremely poor, often with obvious forging faults.

Australian troops in the Pacific made an industry out of fake 'samurai' swords (including spurious blade-tang signatures), selling them to souvenir-seeking GIs. This would account for many peculiar and doubtful variations which are found, especially in the USA.

Plate 65. Infantry in action with a Type 92 7.7mm machine-gun. The officer holds a sword with leather-covered hilt and scabbard. (IWM photograph STT 3306.)

Plate 66. Leather-covered swords. *Left*: with a non-removable leather-covered hilt and a field scabbard. The surrender or transportation label reads 'Kamiya Sadanori, Defence Force'. *Centre*: a shin-guntō with removable lace-up hilt cover. *Right*: a shin-guntō with a removable foul-weather hilt cover secured by a strap and press stud – although they are often tied. (R. Gregory collection).

Plate 67. This leather-covered sword was surrendered to Flying Officer Joss RAF, at Kuala Lumpur Airfield in September 1945. The tassel is tied above the tsuba and the scabbard suspension mount appears to be hinged. Strangely, the officer seems to have the rank patches of a private first class. (Courtesy of D. A. Joss.)

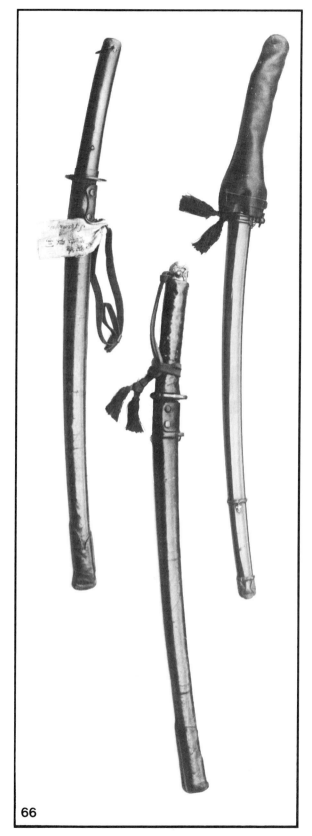

66

67

49

ERSATZ SWORDS

The late 1944 shin-guntō and home defence swords (qv) are regarded in this category, being made in Japan and officially sanctioned.

Another variant examined was probably made in an occupied country – possibly Java, where a steelworks at Sumaran made swords. This distinctive, generally well-made item gives the appearance of an approved design.

The hilt fittings and oval tsuba are all plain blackened steel. One example even appeared to have an indistinct arsenal stamp on the tsuba. A narrow red braiding is bound to expose numerous samē diamonds, reminiscent of the 'rebellion' style. The brass menuki represent an unidentifiable flower. Simulated samē of white embossed canvas material is used, while the steel saru-te is triangular. Retention is by a leather strap and press stud.

The tan-coloured leather field scabbard has a blackened steel throat and one ashi (suspension mount). The poor-quality blade is forged from one piece of steel.

Plates 55-6.

Naval swords

Until 1872, at least, there were no regulation naval swords. Navy officers simply carried a traditional katana in black lacquered scabbard, thrust through the leather service belt.

WILKINSON SWORD COMPANY OFFICERS' PATTERN, 1872

The Wilkinson Sword Company pattern book details a sword, belt and buckle approved by the Imperial Japanese Navy in January 1872. The actual drawings are reproduced in *A Pictorial History of Swords and Bayonets* by R. J. Wilkinson-Latham (1973).

Copied from the British naval pattern of 1846, its guard incorporates a cartouche design of a foul anchor – with a rope entwined around the anchor cross-stay – and two sakura (cherry-blossom). Admirals' swords had a roped edge to the hilt badge that joined the top of the anchor ring.

The sword was accompanied by the standard brass-mounted black leather scabbard. It had a brass half-basket guard, backstrap with lion's head pommel, and a white shagreen grip. A straight blade was used, possibly etched with suitable maritime designs.

Although an approved pattern, no example of this sword has been located. The extent of usage is unknown but it is unlikely that it was carried in large numbers.

Fig. 48.

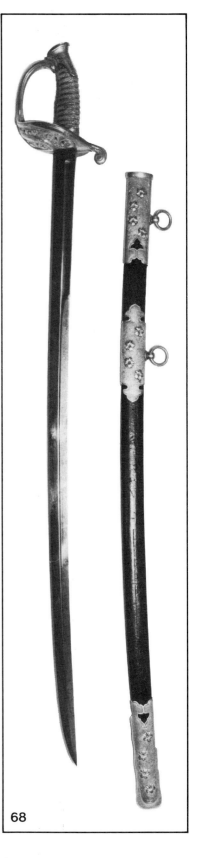

68

Plate 68. A rare naval officers' sword pattern, *c.*1873/4, with gilded brass mounts, a white samē grip and a black leather scabbard. The blade, of unusual style, is hand-forged and signed NAOTAKA – who worked around 1865–8. (R. Gregory collection.)

Plate 69. The hilt of the naval kyu-guntō shown in plate 68. (R. Gregory collection.)

NAVAL KYU-GUNTŌ OFFICERS' PATTERN, ABOUT 1873–4

Late in 1873 or early in 1874, a new sword appeared adopting the European-style pommel of the army kyu-guntō and a curved blade (fig. 25 i).

The backstrap was eliminated and the guard reduced in size, though still engraved with sakura and leaves. The foul anchor design was confined to the pommel, but was simplified by incorporating a single sakura under the anchor cross-stay. A white samē grip was used.

The scabbard design remained unchanged, with three sakura-decorated gilded brass mounts.

It is not known if flag officers had a more elaborate version, or whether non-commissioned officers carried a variant.

Fig. 25; plates 68-9.

MARINES' AND GUNNERS' SWORD PATTERN, ABOUT 1873

1873, or thereabouts, brought the introduction of a sword purely for officers and NCOs of the marines and gunners (marine artillery).

Regular naval officers carried the separate design described in the preceding section.

No example has been found to confirm the following details, which must be regarded as speculative. From fig. 25 ii, the sword appears to have a brass-mounted hilt with a half-basket guard and knucklebow, a European-style angled pommel, and a contoured wire-bound grip without a backstrap. The guard engraving is thought to have been a central sakura with radiating leaves.

The metal scabbard, probably brass, had two roped suspension bands.

Differences may have existed between officer and NCO versions, but the pattern was apparently superseded around 1896 by the naval kyu-guntō.

Fig. 25.

NAVAL KYU-GUNTŌ OFFICERS' PATTERN, ABOUT 1896

According to Sasama's *Nippon-no-Gunso* (1970), the next change came *c*.1896, when amendments were made – including the addition of at least four rank variations (fig. 26). They were all generally similar to the previous model of 1873/74, except for the addition of a backstrap and the reduced size of the pommel. The hilt length was increased to cater for ancestral blades.

Decoration depended on rank. The imperial mon (crest) of the Paulownia imperialis flower (kiri – see Fig. 30 ii) was reserved for flag officers only, sakura (cherryblossom) for remaining officers. The swords of petty officers lacked a backstrap; it is possible that superior petty officers were permitted nanako (stippled or fishroe) finish, while junior petty officers were restricted to plain fittings.

Figs 26-7; plate 71.

NAVAL KYU-GUNTŌ OFFICERS' PATTERN, ABOUT 1914

The previous junior-senior officer pattern (fig. 26 ii) appears to have become standard for all commissioned officers, regardless of rank, shortly before the First World War.

The scabbards may be black leather, lacquered black samē or brown shagreen. Decorative motifs are confined to the sakura. As with all previous models, the sword is retained in the scabbard by a small folding reverse-hilt flap engaging a raised stud on the scabbard locket.

The blades are often ancestral, or sometimes gendaitō, fixed to the hilt by a bamboo peg (mekugi) that passes through the tang. Hilt length varies considerably, depending on tang length.

Petty officers are thought to have carried similar swords with plain brass fittings and mass-produced blades.

Although superseded in the early 1930s by the kai-guntō, these weapons were still carried as a matter of preference by senior officers during the Second World War.

Figs 26, 28; plates 70, 73.

Plate 70. A scarce naval officers' kyu-guntō pattern of *c*.1914, with gilded brass mounts, a white samē grip and a black shagreen-covered scabbard. The knot is an army kyu-guntō pattern. (R. Gregory collection.)

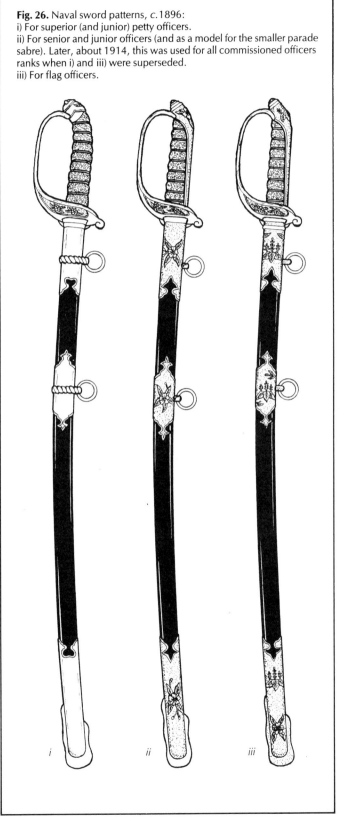

Fig. 25. Naval sword patterns:
i) For commissioned officers, *c.*1874.
ii) For marines and gunnery commissioned officers, *c.*1873.

Fig. 26. Naval sword patterns, *c.*1896:
i) For superior (and junior) petty officers.
ii) For senior and junior officers (and as a model for the smaller parade sabre). Later, about 1914, this was used for all commissioned officers ranks when i) and iii) were superseded.
iii) For flag officers.

Plate 71. Japan's greatest admiral, Count Heihachiro Togo, commander of the Japanese fleet that destroyed the Russians at Tsushima on 27/28 May 1905. He carries a flag officers' kyu-guntō pattern of *c*.1896. (Courtesy of F. J. Stephens).

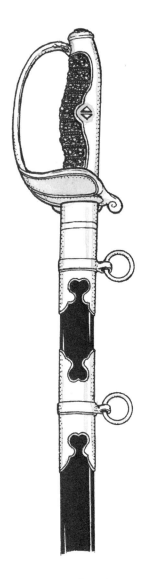

Fig. 27. A Meiji-period naval sword of unusual pattern with a slim 26in blade, sometimes signed and thought to be for naval use. The hilt side-ears and the black samē grip are not normally found on naval swords of kyu-guntō type. The double-triangle hilt badge is similar to that used by the Japanese-owned island of Formosa (Taiwan). A naval dirk has been found with the same badge. Thus, these pieces may have been used by Formosan officers serving in the Japanese forces.

Plate 72. The *first* Japanese sword taken during the Second World War. This kai-guntō belonged to Lieutenant Kazuo Sakamaki IJN, who commanded midget submarine M19, captured off Waimanalo, Oahu, Hawaii, during the Pearl Harbor campaign on 8 December 1941. He was the first prisoner captured by the United States in the war. The blade is not signed. (By courtesy of US Naval Academy Museum, Annapolis; item 42.45.)

Plate 73. Staff officers of the 3rd Army in the Russo-Japanese war. The naval officer standing on the far right holds a naval kyu-guntō, the scabbard of which appears to be fitted with a leather combat cover.

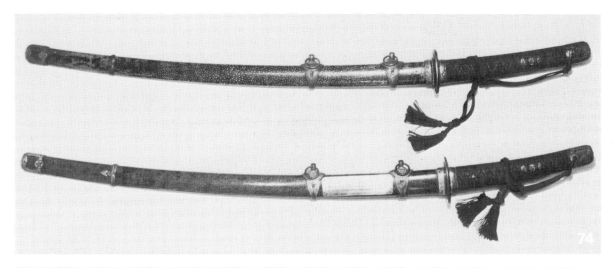

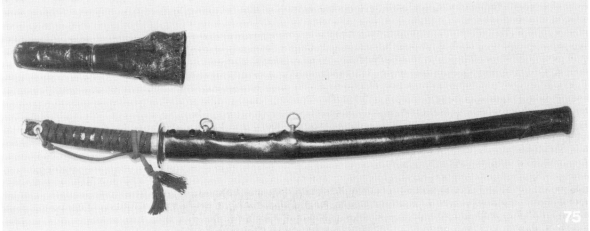

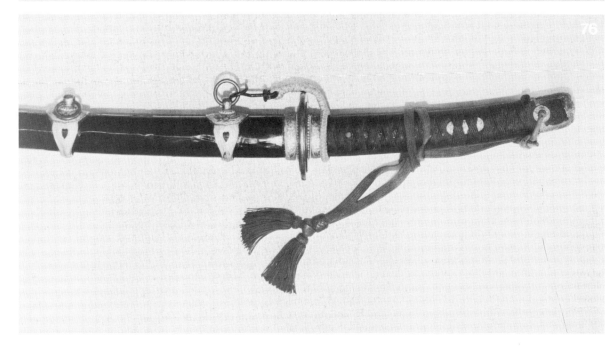

Plate 74. Naval officers' kai-guntō with a black lacquered samē-covered scabbard (top) and one of shagreen (bottom). The brasss plate reads 'Sword surrendered by Captain Tsuneki, Japanese Imperial Navy, to Captain Murphy, Royal Navy, at Mergui, Burma. 19th October 1945'. This was the only naval surrender in the Burma theatre. See plates 114 and 115. (Fuller and Gregory collections).

Plate 75. A naval officers' kai-guntō with a black leather combat cover on the scabbard and a foul-weather hilt cover. (R. Gregory collection.)

Plate 76. This naval officers' kai-guntō has a black lacquered scabbard. The retention system of rope-and-hook is very rare. (R. Gregory collection).

Plate 77. Pictured while signing the Japanese surrender of Hong Kong at Government House on 2 September 1945, Major-General Umekichi Okada (sitting) has a shin-guntō with a blade by Tadayoshi I or II of Hizen, 1600–50. Vice-Admiral Ruitaro Fujita (far right) holds his kai-guntō with a blade signed 'Made at the Tenshozan Forge, June 1942'. Both swords are now in the National Maritime Museum. (Private photo collection.)

NAVAL KAI-GUNTŌ OFFICERS' PATTERN

To conform with the army, a new sword pattern – based on the traditional tachi (slung sword) – was introduced to the navy in the early 1930s.

Its hilt of brown tape, often flat (fig. 9 iii), is bound over black samē and fitted with gilded brass or copper kabuto-gane (pommel) and fuchi (collar). The gilt menuki features three sakura in circles. An ovoid (naga-maru) tsuba, made of plain dark blue-black shakudo-finished copper or brass, has large shakudo dai-seppa on either side. These are of similar ovoid shape, engraved in the form of sun rays with alternating plain and nanako (fishroe) finish. Occasional examples may feature alternating brass and copper rays.

The blades are mass-produced, hand forged (gendaitō) or ancestral. The swords are either push fits or retained in their scabbards by the standard push button spring clip used with army shin-guntō.

The scabbard consists of a wood liner covered with blue-black polished and lacquered shagreen, samē or plain black lacquer. The shagreen, or sharkskin, has the appearance of small diamonds; the samē, rayskin, appears as circular inlays of ivory on a plain black ground. Five gilded brass or copper fittings, decorated to match the hilt, include two ashi (suspension mounts) that differ in design from the shin-guntō pattern (fig. 10 ii). Single ashi field scabbards are known, but are rare.

Field scabbards of blue-black leather over a wooden liner are sometimes found, as are combat covers.

No rank distinction was made – even with the tassel, which was plain brown.

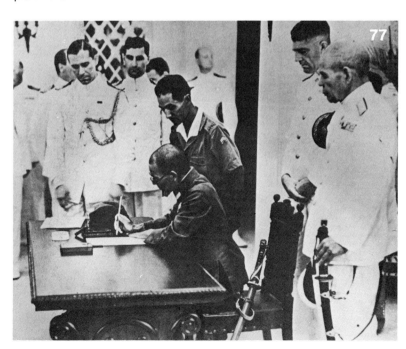

These swords are relatively scarce, as naval losses during the Second World War were extremely high: nearly three-quarters of the navy's ships were lost. The kai-guntō were carried by regular naval officers aboard ship and by most officers assigned to land garrison units.

A naval lieutenant confirmed that his kai-guntō with oil tempered blade cost 80 yen ($18.40 or £9.13s.4d in 1941). As his pay was only 120 yen per month, his sword was an expensive item.

Figs 9, 10; plates 72, 74-7.

NAVAL NON-COMMISSIONED OFFICERS' KAI-GUNTŌ PATTERN

Petty officers are said to have carried a sword closely resembling the officers' kai-guntō. This has not yet been verified, as most group photographs show only commissioned officers with swords. However, the National Maritime Museum has one (item no. 358) which is believed to have come from a petty officer on a Japanese warship at Singapore in September 1945: the cruisers *Takao* and *Myoko*, or the destroyer *Kamikaze*.

Plate 79. A naval officers' parade sabre carried until the end of the Second World War. It has brass mounts, a white samē grip and (on this example) a brown-lacquered shagreen scabbard. Note the similarity to the naval officers' kyu-guntō pattern of *c.*1914. (R. Fuller collection.)

Plate 80. Two naval parade sabres.
Top: made to special order, this rare example incorporates the Paulownia (kiri) mon on the scabbard locket used by flag officers, *c.*1896.
Bottom: the standard parade sabre with knot.
(B. P. Williams collection.)

Plate 78. A crude sword with plain brass fittings and a machine-made blade. It is reputed to be a naval NCOs' kai-guntō, but may only be an Indian or native-made wartime copy sold to Allied troops. (R. Fuller collection.)

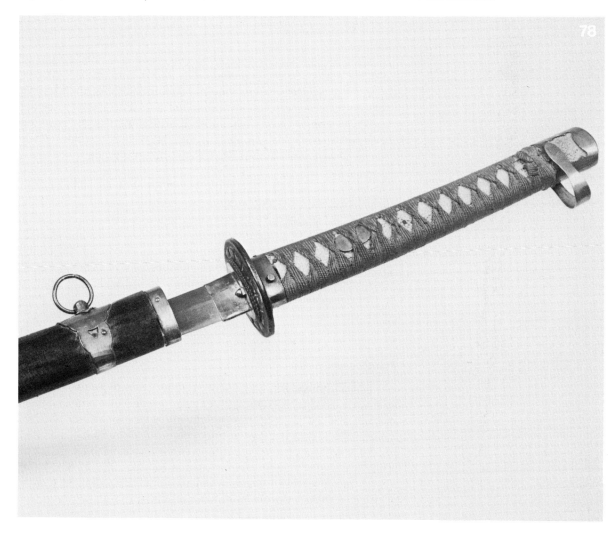

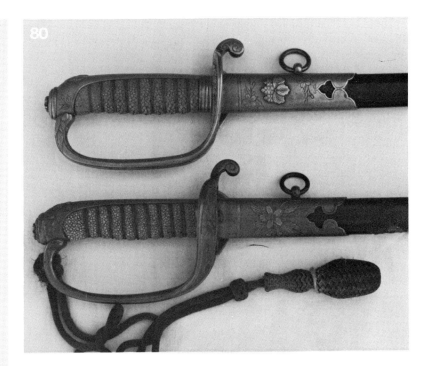

A yellow or light tan cotton binding is bound over several pieces of white samē. The blackened steel tsuba and dai-seppa are roughly cast integrally, simulating the officers' design; brass habaki and first seppa are also integral. The hilt and scabbard fittings are plain brass, poorly shaped, hammered and pinned to the wooden base. The scabbard covering is a thin blue-black leather. Blade retention is achieved by a push button and spring clip.

The mass-produced blade has a rounded back-edge, not found in Japanese swords, and a poorly defined ridge line (shinogi). It is generally glued to the hilt, which cannot be removed.

It has been suggested that this sword is an ersatz or emergency officers' pattern, but the large amount of brass seems to discredit this claim. Since workmanship is so poor and not typical of the Japanese, the possibility must be considered that they are no more than Indian or native-made souvenirs sold to Allied servicemen who thought they were buying genuine captured swords.

Plate 78.

NAVAL PARADE SABRE

A smaller, lightweight version of the senior and junior officers' naval kyu-guntō of c.1896 was later adopted by all commissioned officer ranks. Its narrow mass-produced blade sometimes has an acid-etched yakiba (tempered edge).

The gilded brass hilt and scabbard fittings match the larger naval kyu-guntō design. Their scabbards are also a copy of the large pattern, black leather, lacquered black samē or lacquered brown shagreen. Retention is by the folding reverse-hilt flap and a raised locket stud.

They may have been introduced as early as 1896, as one example has been found with the Paulownia imperialis (kiri) mon used by flag officers. The decoration is normally confined to the sakura. They are likely to have been carried throughout the Second World War

Things have gone full circle, since the Wilkinson Sword Company apparently supplies an identical sword to the modern Japanese navy. This would have the manufacturer's logo and a blade etched with designs unknown on pre-war examples.

Fig. 28; plates 79, 80.

Fig. 28. This is the standard backstrap design for all ranks of naval officers' post-1914 model kyu-guntō swords. Naval parade sabre decoration is identical. The silver mon on this example is that of the Hasebe and Mori families.

Civil swords

DIPLOMATIC CORPS SWORD PATTERN

The history of diplomatic swords is obscure, apparently with only one authorised pattern. Introduction is conjectural, but possibly around 1873 when the similar, but less ornate army dress sword appeared. Diplomatic swords were worn on full dress occasions by Japanese members of the diplomatic corps (kakkoku-koshi) at least until 1941.

The richly engraved gilded-brass hilt fittings consist of large downward curving shellguards, the obverse featuring a engraved or pierced Paulownia imperialis (kiri). A knucklebow with raised phoenix-head quillon, and a spherical pommel with elongated tang button are also notable. The gilded-wire bound white samē grip has decorated side straps. The swords of diplomats whose appointments had been personally approved by the Emperor, called 'chokunin', had a kiri design featuring seven central flowers and five on each side (fig. 30 ii). Those who received standard appointments, the 'sonin', had five central flowers with three on each side.

The slim ½in wide straight blade is unique among Japanese swords in that it has etched designs on each side (fig. 29). This is probably restricted to swords of 'chokunin' diplomats.

The black lacquer or leather scabbard has two gilded brass mounts, the upper having a obverse frog stud in the form of a leaf while the lower terminates in a ball finial.

The scabbard is suspended by means of a black velvet V-shaped frog hung from a white watered-silk shoulder belt.

A variation exists with a curved ancestral blade. Its black lacquered scabbard has richly decorated mounts, including two suspension bands for use with a belt and slings. The most unusual feature is two full-length strengthening straps. The hilt style is reminiscent of the army kyu-guntō, with a backstrap and white samē grip, but incorporates the diplomatic-pattern shellguards.

As the diplomats' sword is rare, the version with ancestral blade must rate as extremely rare.

Fig. 29; plates 81-5.

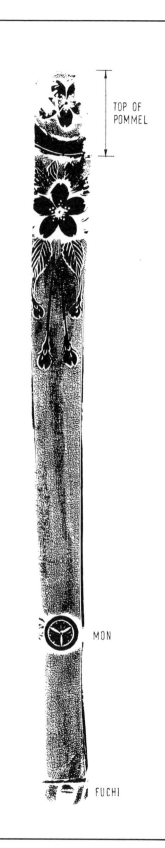

TOP OF POMMEL

MON

FUCHI

Plate 81. This rare diplomatic corps dress sword has an etched blade and gilded brass fittings ('chokunin' rank version). The black-lacquered scabbard is carried in a black velvet frog with a white watered-silk shoulder strap. Note the gold bullion dress knot. (R. Gregory collection.)

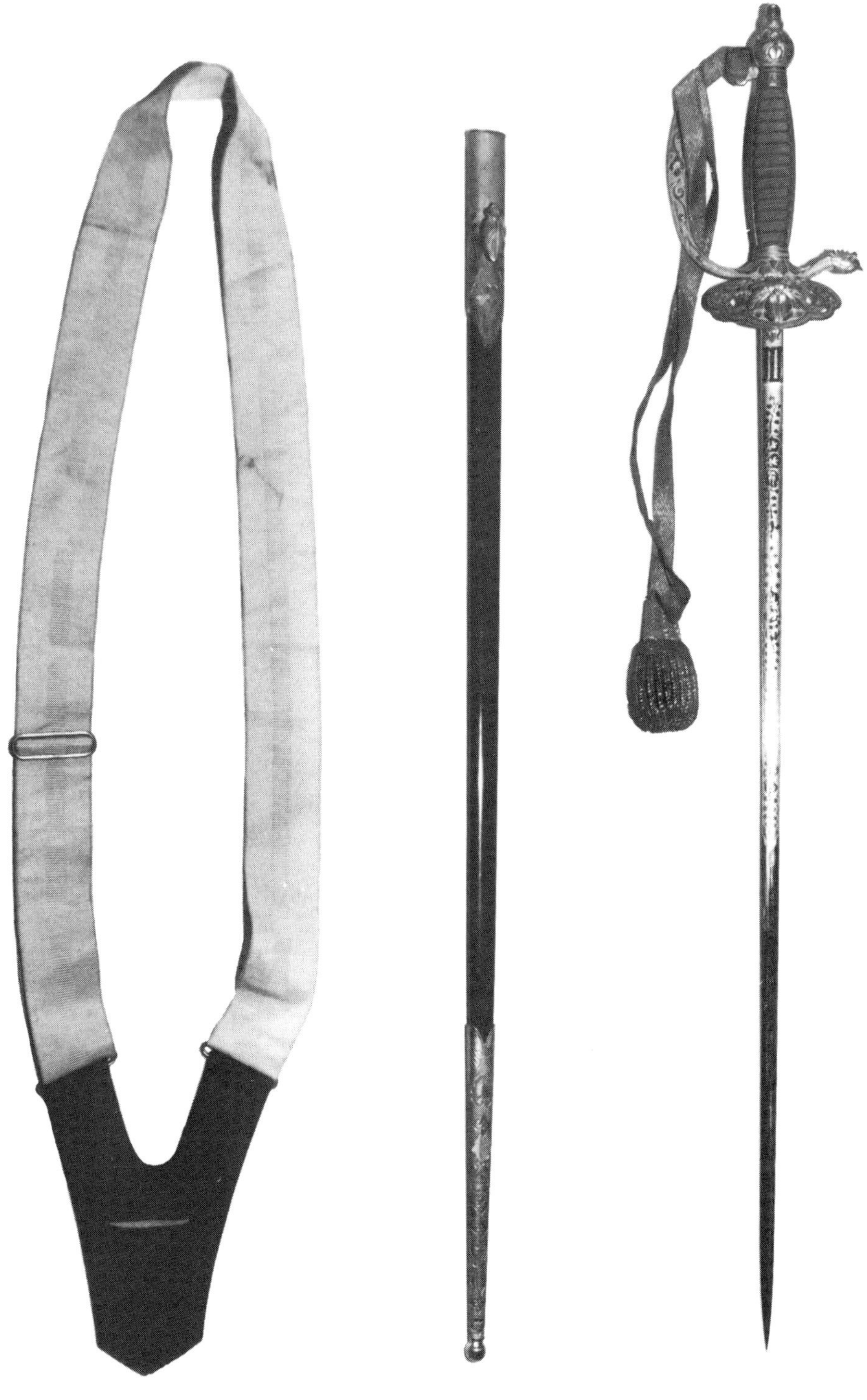

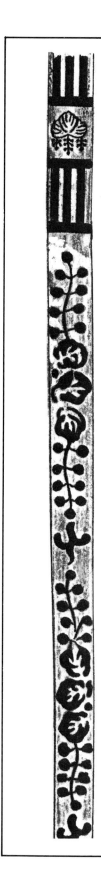

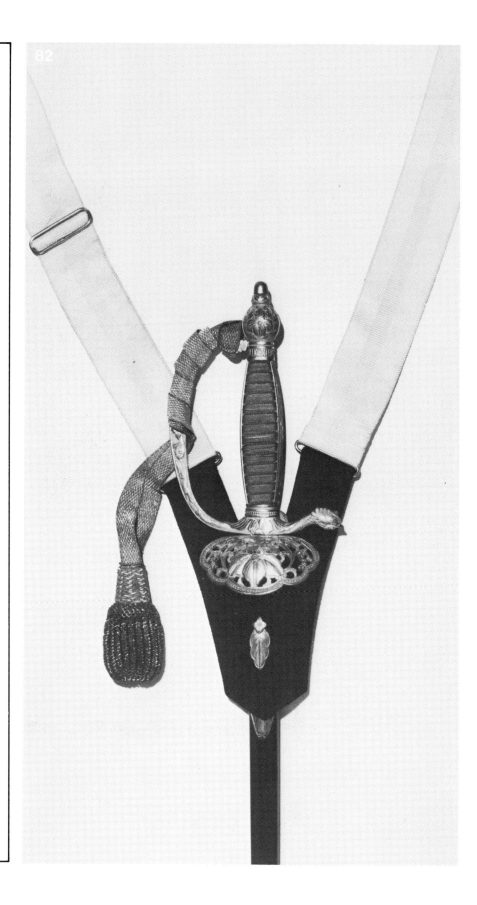

Fig. 29. The blade etching pattern of the diplomatic sword.

Plate 82. The obverse hilt design of a rare diplomatic corps dress sword. The quillon forms the head of a phoenix. The pommel and guard are decorated with the Paulownia imperialis (kiri) associated with the royal family. A leaf-like frog stud protrudes from the black-velvet frog. (R. Gregory collection.)

Plate 83. A very rare variation of the diplomatic corps dress sword, made for an ancestral curved blade. There are finely-crafted gilded mounts, a white same grip, a black-lacquered scabbard with side straps, and two ornate suspension mounts. This example has the Paulownia (kiri) mon used by 'chokunin' ranks. (K. Hostler collection.)

Plate 84. The reverse of hilt shown in plate 83. The large folding guard is in the downward position, engaging a raised stud on the scabbard locket. (K. Hostler collection.)

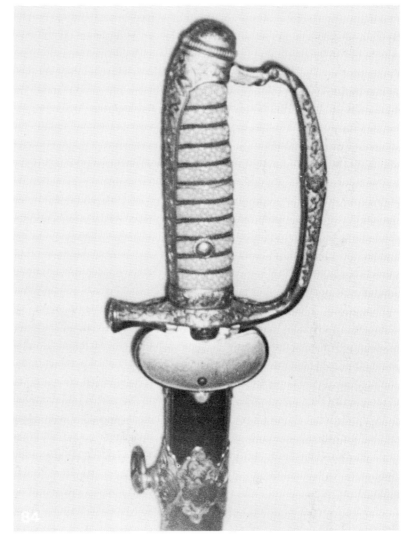

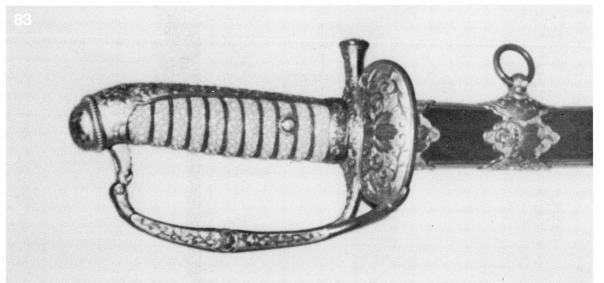

THE LATE MINISTER OKUBO.

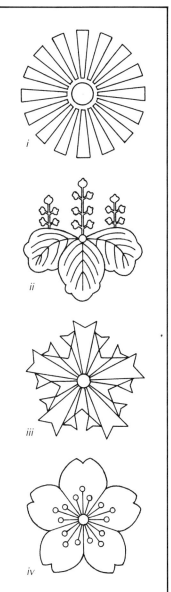

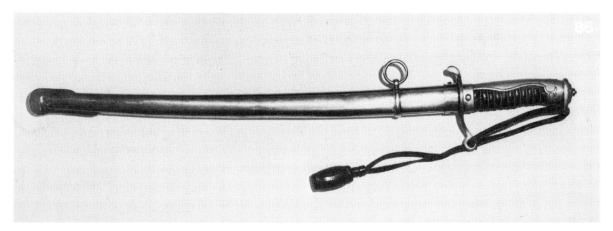

POLICE SWORDS

The evolution of police swords has yet to be properly traced, but can probably be assessed from examples in a private collection. Such swords are clearly recognisable, no matter what their pattern, by the large police badge (figs 30 iii, 31) on the upper backstrap.

The first pattern may have been a short hanger or dirk introduced at the beginning of the Meiji era. Its brass hilt consists of a flattened pommel, a backstrap with badge, a slightly inverted crossguard and a wire-bound white samē grip. The example quoted has a hand-forged blade and nickel-plated scabbard. The sword is held in the scabbard by a push-button spring clip.

The second pattern appears to be a development of the first. It is much longer, with a black samē grip; again, the backstrap has the police badge. The inverted crossguard has a ring in the front while the pommel incorporates a smaller one – for a brown leather sword knot, rather than a chain guard. The blade and the scabbard are identical with the earlier pattern.

A sabre similar to the army parade pattern may have been carried, but no example has been located for verification. Police swords are scarce.

Figs 30-1; plates 86-9.

Fig. 30. Sword badges:
i) The chrysanthemum (kiku) found on the hilts of general officers' kyu-guntō swords.
ii) The Paulownia imperialis (kiri) found on flag officers' naval swords made after 1896, and diplomatic corps dress swords.
iii) The police badge found on sword hilts.
iv) The cherryblossom (sakura) found on most military swords.

Fig. 31. The difference between police and army parade sabre back straps.
i) The cast badge on the back of a police sabre.
ii) The partly decorated backstrap of an army parade sabre. Note the unidentified silver mon near the base.

Plate 85. Government minister Okubo with a diplomatic dress sword and uniform, c.1904–5.

Plate 86. An early (Meiji-period) short police sword-pattern with a brass hilt, a steel scabbard and a brown leather knot. (R. Gregory collection.)

i   *ii*

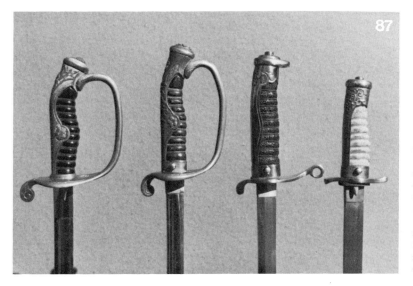

Plate 87. Army parade and police sabres.
Left to right:
i) A standard junior army officers' parade sabre with a horn grip.
ii) A rare army general officers' parade sabre with a horn grip. Note the spring-clip retention and habaki, both uncommon on parade sabres.
iii) A police sword with a black samē grip. It is probably from the Meiji period, superseding the next item.
iv) A police Meiji-period dirk with a white samē grip. Possibly the first pattern.
(B. P. Williams collection.)

Plate 88. Army parade and police sabres. The backstraps of swords in plate 87. Note the general officers' kiku (chrysanthemum) badge on the second from the left, and police badges on the two on the right. (B. P. Williams collection.)

Plate 89. The backstrap of a Meiji-period short police sword, clearly showing the police badge. (H. Gopstein collection.)

Plate 90. An unidentified Meiji-period sword, possibly for civil officials, with brass mounts, a samē grip and a steel scabbard. This example has an unsigned Kotō-period (pre-1596) blade. (R. Gregory collection.)

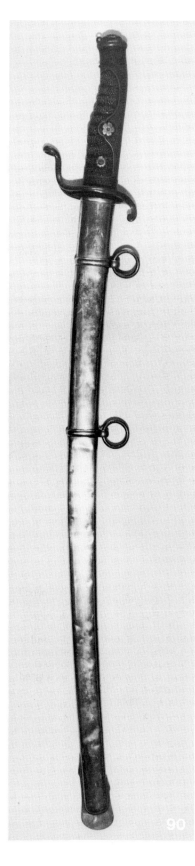

UNIDENTIFIED SWORDS

The four swords described below are said to be Meiji-era patterns used by civil officials – presumably with military connections – but no contemporaneous photographs have provided confirmation. Like the Meiji police swords, leather (or possibly bullion) knots would be used rather than chain guards. All these swords are scarce.

Type I. The hand-engraved copper hilt of this sword features sakura and leaves, plus a crescent moon and a sun or full moon among clouds. The domed pommel should have a small loose ring held in a loop, while the small decorated inverted crossguard has a large raised ring unusually set in a horizontal plane. The grip is wire-bound black samē. A hand-forged kotō period blade fits into a plated steel scabbard with two ashi (suspension mounts). The overall length is 30½in.

The high quality indicates use by a person of high rank. The army is not known to have carried such patterns. (Fig. 32 i; plate 90.)

Type II. Similar to (I) but less ornate, this sword also features two hilt rings; the crossguard ring is in the normal vertical plane, in common with police swords. The hilt fittings are plain brass, with a backstrap, and the grip is black samē. Once again, a hand-forged blade is fitted. The black leather scabbard has a wooden liner, and the four brass mounts include two suspension bands. Sakura appear only twice, on the menuki (hilt ornament on the securing peg) and pommel. (Fig. 32 ii; plate 91.)

Type III. A photograph of another version of this sword has been seen, differing in that the scabbard is painted metal and the rear of the hilt has a small folding guard that engages with a scabbard stud as on naval kyu-guntō. The tang button takes the form of a sakura and the upper backstrap is engraved with sakura and leaves.

A variant examined has a 23⅜in straight blade, no backstrap, the Koishikawa arsenal mark, and the number 80 stamped on the pommel.

The 'Type III' sword may have been for officers, and the variant for NCOs. Both may have naval connections. (Plate 94.)

Type IV. The most ornate of these unidentified swords examined has a gilded brass hilt and matching scabbard fittings decorated with engraved sakura, leaves and scrolls. The hilt fittings consist of a white samē grip, a pommel mounted with a sakura and a small swivel ring, a backstrap, and an inverted crossguard. The crossguard, unusually, lacks a ring. The curved ancestral blade of wakizashi length fits into a black leather scabbard, whose three mounts include two suspension bands. The overall length is 33in.

The quality is such that use by a person of high rank, with army connections, is most likely. (Plates 92-3.)

Figs 32 i and ii; plates 90–4.

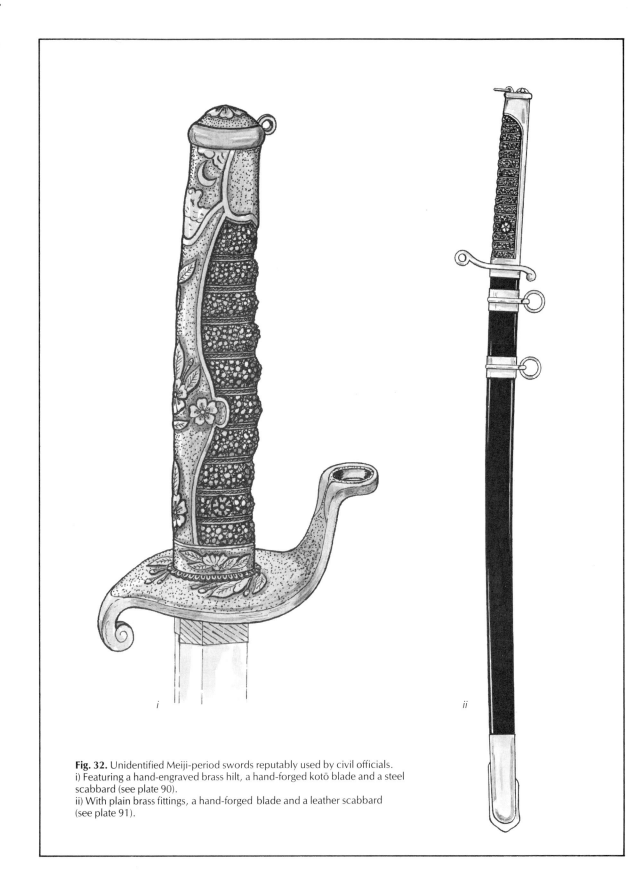

Fig. 32. Unidentified Meiji-period swords reputably used by civil officials.
i) Featuring a hand-engraved brass hilt, a hand-forged kotō blade and a steel scabbard (see plate 90).
ii) With plain brass fittings, a hand-forged blade and a leather scabbard (see plate 91).

i

ii

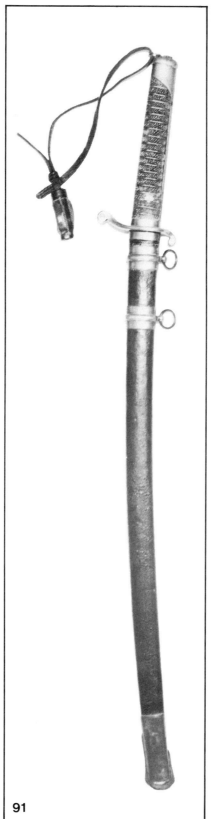

Plate 91. An unidentified Meiji-period sword, said to be a civil official's. It has brass mounts, a black samē grip and a black leather scabbard. (R. Gregory collection.)

Plate 92. An ornate and scarce variation of an unidentified Meiji-period sword, which lacks a crossguard ring. There are gilded brass fittings and a leather scabbard for the ancestral blade. This sword was reputedly for a civil official, probably of high rank. (R. Lindus collection.)

Plate 93. The guard of the unidentified Meiji-period sword shown in plate 92. (R. Lindus collection.)

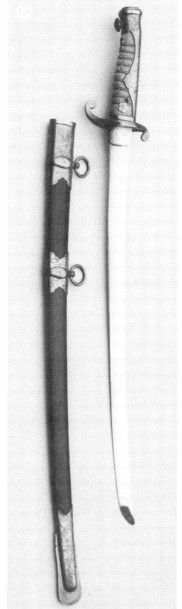

91

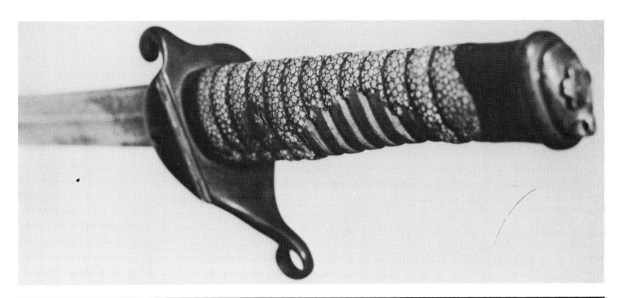

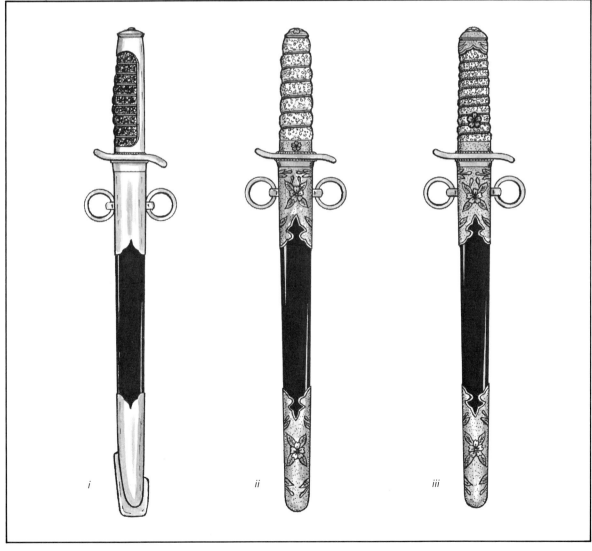

i   ii   iii

Dirks

NAVAL DIRKS

Plate 94. The reverse of an unidentified Meiji-period sword with a white samē grip and brass mounts. The folding guard may indicate naval use. The pommel has stamped numbers and the Koishikawa (Tōkyō) Arsenal symbol, possibly indicative of official issue. (R. Gregory collection.)

Fig. 33. Naval dirks:
i) A 1873 superior petty officers' and junior commissioned officers' dirk, as modified in 1883.
ii) The 1883 commissioned officers' dirk.
iii) A modified 1883 commissioned officers' dirk.

WILKINSON PATTERN, ABOUT 1872

The Wilkinson Sword Company may have provided a dirk *c.*1872, based on the then-current British pattern of 1856 with the lengthened blade of 1870. The Japanese variation would have differed only in the design of the hilt badge, with a sakura (cherryblossom) in place of the foul anchor. No example has been located and official adoption is doubtful.

1873 PATTERN

According to Commander W. E. May and P. G. W. Annis, in *Swords for Sea Service* (1970), an officially-approved pattern was introduced on 15 December 1873 for superior petty officers and junior commissioned officers (fig. 33).

The single-edged blade is mounted in a hilt featuring a wire-bound black samē grip on a wooden base. A habaki (blade collar) is normally absent. The plain gilt-brass fittings consist of a short straight crossguard, a backstrap and a pommel. The scabbards are brown or black leather, or possibly polished samē, with two gilded brass mounts. The scabbard is suspended from two loose opposing rings, although those on earlier examples are thought to have been fixed. A drag may also be lacking on early items. Slight modifications were made in 1883.

Junior petty officers carried the same pattern, but with steel mounts. Examples of both types are rare.

Fig. 33.

1883 PATTERN

Swords for Sea Service records the introduction of a new pattern on 26 October 1883 for all senior commissioned officers including flag officers (admirals) (fig. 33 ii). The 1873 pattern was retained for superior petty officers and junior commissioned officers, virtually unchanged except for a domed pommel and inverted crossguard (fig. 33 i). It is not known when this modified pattern was phased out.

The 1883 senior officers' design was more traditional, resembling a tantō. It and, in particular, the later modified form are the most frequently encountered navy dirks — being carried throughout the Second World War.

A single-edged fullered blade is mounted in a tapering white or, in rare cases, black samē-covered grip with spirally wrapped gilded wire binding. All fittings are gilt-finished brass, consisting of a domed pommel, a fuchi and a short inverted crossguard. The fuchi usually has a raised sakura, as has the pommel top, though a star is sometimes found. Blades are mass-produced or hand-forged.

The scabbards are blue-black leather, polished black samē or brown shagreen, with matching gilt-finished fittings decorated with sakura and leaves. Occasionally, they may be plain with stippled finish.

A rare example with a backstrap may be an early transitional model.

Figs 33 i and ii; plates 95-6, 98.

MODIFIED 1883 PATTERN

The most commonly encountered navy dirk is a modified version of the 1883 model that is possibly just a variation. It is seen in photographs as early as 1904 and continued in production until the end of the Second World War. The pommel size was increased with the sakura, previously on the fuchi, repositioned on each side of the hilt to serve as menuki covering the male and female hilt retaining screws (fig. 33 iii). The single hanging rings found on some examples are thought to be later variants.

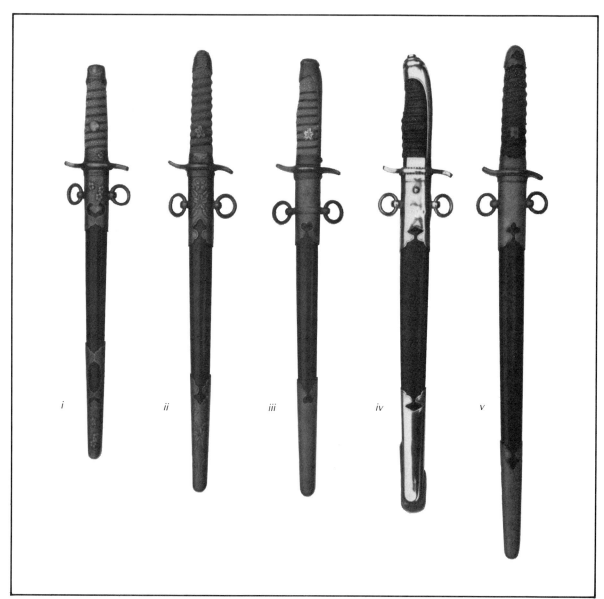

i   *ii*   *iii*   *iv*   *v*

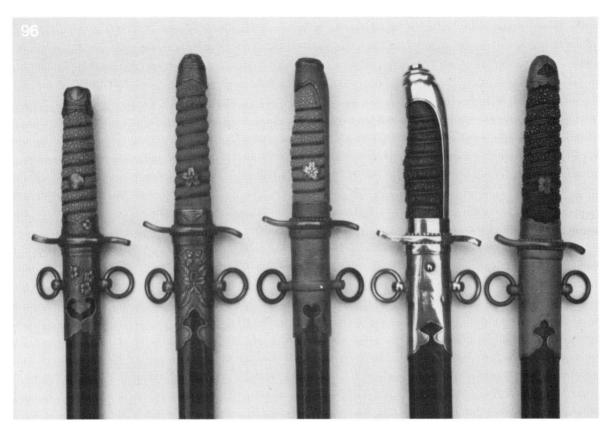

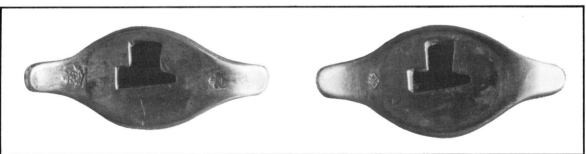

Plate 97. Naval dirk crossguards showing arsenal or acceptance stamps. (B. P. Williams collection.)

These dirks were worn by all commissioned officers. Many variations are encountered in fittings, decoration and quality of workmanship. Examples made towards the end of the Second World War often had simulated samē grips made from a plastic or composition material. The mounts are badly formed, and may even be found with copper-finished white plastic or celluloid crossguards.

The modified 1883 pattern is still in production for the modern Japanese navy. Unfortunately, there are no obvious differences between pre-1945 and modern pieces except for the 'newness' of the latter and a modern manufacturer's logo.

The blades on all models of naval dirk are generally mass-produced, single edged and grooved, although examples with old hand-forged tantō blades are occasionally found.

Fig. 33; plates 95-8.

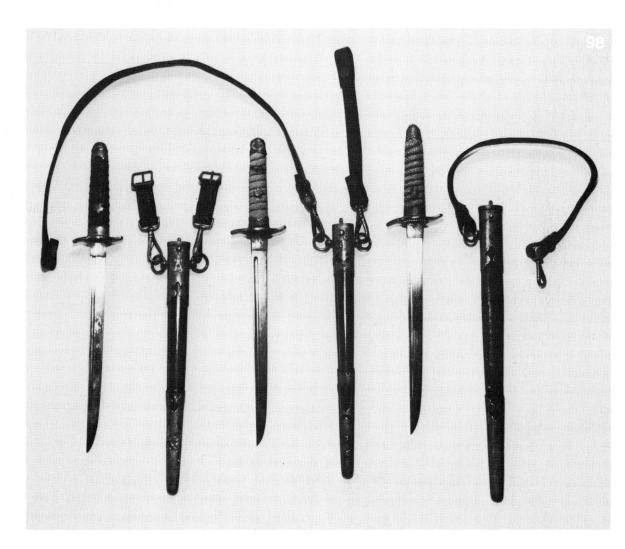

ARMY DIRKS

Army officers are not known to have had an official dirk. However, some carried traditional civilian tantō with leather combat cover, possibly in preference to a heavy sword. These tantō are rarely found and it is unlikely that carrying them was common practice.

It has been suggested that army cadet schools had regulation-pattern daggers or even short swords, but confirmation is lacking.

Plate 57.

KAMIKAZE DIRKS

The legendary kamikaze (divine wind) special attack corps was formed from volunteer pilots who deliberately crashed their planes or Okhas (piloted bombs) into enemy shipping. The first operational attack occurred on 25 October 1944 and continued until their suspension before the surrender. The overall military effect was minimal but, despite high Japanese losses, they achieved great psychological success by terrifying allied naval personnel.

A kamikaze pilot could, if he wished, carry a small aikuchi (a dagger without a guard) to cut his jugular vein during the last moments before hitting the target. It is doubtful if he ever had time.

Plates 99, 100.

The daggers are traditional in appearance with a slightly curved, single-edged and often fullered blade, mass-produced or hand-forged but always fitted with a habaki (blade collar). They sometimes bear engraving such as 'Go forth and conquer and your deeds will be recited in history'.

The dark polished rosewood grip and scabbard have bone or ivory collars. Black lacquered scabbards are occasionally found. The blades can be separated from the hilt by removing a bamboo securing peg (mekugi). A small hole at the hilt-top receives a wrist cord.

The leather combat cover that encases both hilt and scabbard, being hung from the neck by a long loop of cord, is usually missing.

Kamikaze dirks are obviously very rare – most went up in flames, although a few survived in Japan and others were recovered from planes that did not explode.

Naval kaiten (manned suicide torpedo) pilots were given a suicide dirk at a special ceremony before setting out. No example has been located, but is thought to have been similar to the kamikaze pattern.

Similar daggers with coloured tassels are frequently seen, but are tourist souvenirs or letter-openers. Mass-produced, without a habaki, they can fool the inexperienced collector.

Plates 99, 100.

Plate 98. Three naval dirk variations, showing the scarce black samē grip (left) and a single suspension mount (right). The suspension straps are black leather. The blades are machine-made. (R. Gregory collection.)

Fig. 34. A brass mounted dirk with a painted imitation tortoise-shell grip. Often described as a Japanese army or naval dagger it is, in fact, a Nationalist Chinese army dress dagger.

Plate 99. Two rare kamikaze pilots' dirks. Note the protective linen bag (left). The example on the right is complete with a wrist cord, and its brown-leather combat cover has a neck-cord. (R. Gregory collection.)

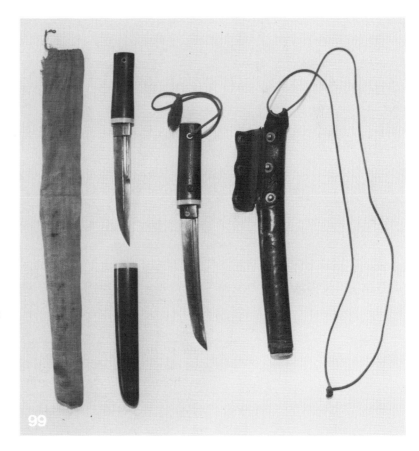

99

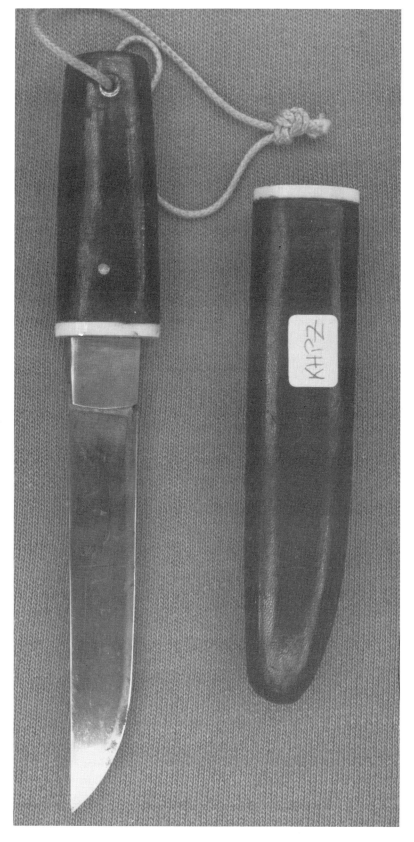

Plate 100. A kamikaze dirk variant. The black leather-covered hilt and scabbard bear the impressed number 85. The collars are celluloid, and the blade is hand-forged. (H. Gopstein collection.)

Blades

It is beyond the scope of this book to discuss blade-making and swordsmiths in detail, other than to summarize the types encountered in military sword mounts. Lists and oshigata (tang rubbings) of swordsmiths of the shōwa period, with Japanese and English readings, are shown in *Swordsmiths of Japan 1926–1945* by the authors – printed and distributed privately, 1983.

ANCESTRAL BLADES

Dating prior to 1867, these come from samurai swords rehilted in military mounts by their owners or for sale to those wishing better-quality blades. There were literally thousands of smiths who made them throughout Japanese swordsmithing history. Specialist books should be consulted.

The blades were hand-forged in various ways to produce a grain (hada) and a tempered edge (yakiba). Along the yakiba is a misty white line, called the hamon. Found in various forms, it is composed of martensite crystals called nie (fine) and nioi (very fine). Either or both may be present. Tempering is done in water. The hardness of the top, side and inner steels may vary, while quality fluctuated considerably according to the skill of the smith. Polishing was done by hand.

MACHINE MADE

Produced from single bars of steel, these blades are machine-hammered and polished or plated. No grain is present and any yakiba is false, being acid-etched. The whole blade may be tempered in oil.

対 綉 鋼

TAI-SHŪ-KŌ

'Anti-rust-steel' or stainless steel blades made by the Tenshozan Company in Kamakura often have this inscribed on their tangs. Sold through the company's own retail outlet, they are associated with Shōwa-period kai-guntō swords only. They are classified as machine-made.

Stainless steel blades from other sources may be found with all patterns of military sword.

MURATŌ

This process was invented by Tsuneyoshi Murata around the turn of the twentieth century. The blade is basically a one-piece machine-made pattern. A yakiba was produced by tempering in oil but failed to produce any nie or nioi along the hamon. Some handwork was involved in tempering and polishing, resulting in a product classifiable as superior machine-made.

満 鐵

MANTETSU

These blades were forged by inserting a soft steel inner core into a pipe of Manchurian-made or western steel (often scrap railway lines). The characters are inscribed on the tang of Shōwa-period blades probably manufactured at the Mukden Arsenal, Manchuria, and by the South Manchurian Arsenal (Second Mukden Arsenal constructed in 1939 and under the direct control of the Japanese Army from Tōkyō). Mantetsu blades are classifiable as superior machine-made.

GENDAITŌ

These hand-forged blades have been made in the traditional manner since 1868. The best of modern sword blades, but purists nonetheless consider them inferior to kotō and shinto examples because the yakiba (tempered edge) is said to be weaker in comparison. Nioi and nie are produced by water tempering. A grain (hada) is also present.

There have been some excellent gendaitō smiths, a few of the very best even being honoured with the title 'Living National Treasure' after the Second World War. Perhaps the best group comprised those who worked at the Yasukuni Shrine, their blades now being appreciated and much-sought.

SHŌWATŌ

All blades produced since 1926 should be properly termed 'shōwatō'. Though often used only for machine-made blades, it must encompass all types – including shōwa-period gendaitō.

One identifying feature is a length of unsharpened or blunt blade in front of the habaki. Known as ubu-ha, it appears on most shōwa blades but is usually no more than 1in long. It is usually claimed that blades of all periods originally had this feature, but that after three or four repolishes it disappeared. Shōwa blades, of course, will not have been repolished. However, some 19th and very early 20th century blades (which have definitely not been repolished) also reportedly lack this feature.

Signatures are often careless in the formation of the characters (kanji) and are frequently in a 'chippy style' of small arrowhead strokes. Tangs should only be lightly rusted with one or, at most, two peg holes because rehilting is unlikely unless it has been done since 1945.

POLISHING

The polishing of blades was an art in itself, being undertaken by specialist craftsmen who produced the mirror-like finish by hand with special graded stones. Machine-made blades were normally machine polished, though some were partly or wholly hand finished. From about 1942, women polishers were also employed in the sword centres and arsenals controlled by the military authorities.

MANUFACTURING CENTRES

The most prolific true arsenal appears to be Kokura, with Tōkyō and Ōsaka close behind. All three mass-produced machine-made blades.

As demand grew, places like Seki in Nōshū (Mino) province again thrived as production centres. Here, all types of blades – including gendaitō – were produced at separate forges. In late 1941 or early 1942 the army blade department took control, establishing a central collecting and assembly centre in Seki where all locally-produced blades were sent for distribution. Thus, the popular term 'Seki arsenal' is a misconception: it should really be 'Seki forges'. The common Seki stamp represents army inspection and acceptance.

Places such as Takayama and Okayama started prison forges around 1941, utilising convict labour under the direction of qualified swordsmiths.

YASUKUNI SHRINE SMITHS

Yasukuni Shrine on Kudan Hill, outside Tōkyō, was built by the Emperor Mutsuhito (Meiji) as the official repository of the souls of all military war dead.

On 9 July 1933, the Nippontō Tanrenkai (Japanese sword forging and tempering society) was officially established at the shrine to restore the art of traditional blade making. Regarded as very important, it was opened by war minister Araki and other military dignitaries at a special ceremony.

Instructors and pupils who became qualified swordsmiths were honoured by being given the right to use the character YASU— 靖 —in their professional names. When working at the shrine they used a two-character signature and date only. The forge was closed in 1945 before the surrender.

The following list tabulates some of the smiths involved:

Yasutoku 靖徳 (Kajiyama Tokutaro), an instructor and perhaps the most important of these smiths. His students:

i) **Kotani Yasunori** 靖憲 nephew of Yasutoku. He made blades for admirals of the fleet and field marshals.

ii) **Yasutoshi** 靖利 son of Yasutoku.

iii) **Yasuyoshi** (Ajiki Haruyoshi) 靖吉. He may have been a pupil of (i), but this has not been substantiated.

iv) **Yasumune** 靖宗 .

v) **Yasuoki** 靖興 .

Yasumitsu 靖光 (Ikeda Kazumitsu), an instructor. His students:

i) **Yasushige** 靖繁 (Abe Shigeo).

ii) **Yatsukuwa Yasutake** 靖武 .

iii) **Yasunobu** 靖延 (family name Murakami).

iv) **Yasuaki** 靖要 .

Yasuhiro 靖廣 (Miyaguchi Ikkansai Toshihiro), an instructor. His students have not been located.

Plate 101.

Plate 101. Soldiers returning from worship at the Yasukuni Shrine, 1937. The Emperor himself worshipped there each year on Army Day (the commemoration of the Russo-Japanese War).

i) Koishikawa (Tōkyō) Arsenal (c.1870–1935) and Kokura Arsenal symbol (1929–45) (S,B).
ii) An unidentified private company under Kokura Arsenal supervision.
iii) National Denki [National Electric] Company; pre-1941 (B).
iv) National Denki Company under Kokura Arsenal supervision (B).
v) Jinsen (Inchon) Arsenal symbol, Korea (1920s–45) (B).
vi) Nagoya Arsenal symbol (1923–45) (B).
vii) Toyada Jidoshoki Seisakusho (Toyada Automatic Loom Works Ltd), Nagoya (B).
viii) Uncertain; reputed to be Howa Jyuko in Ōsaka (B).
ix) An unidentified private company operating under Nagoya Arsenal supervision (B).
x) An unidentified private company operating under Nagoya Arsenal supervision (B).
xi) Nambu Works under Nagoya Arsenal supervision.
xii) Nagoya Arsenal, first series.
xiii) Nagoya Arsenal, second series.
xiv) Mukden Arsenal symbol, Manchuria (1930s–45) (B).
xv) Unidentified (B).
xvi) Seki Forges, Mino (Nōshū) province. An army acceptance stamp, post-1942 (S).
xvii) Unidentified; appears to be associated with Kokura Arsenal (S).
xviii) Unidentified. Appears to be an army acceptance stamp with no specific location (S).
xix) Control stamp of Mukden Arsenal, Manchuria (1930s–45) (S).
xx) Tenshōzan in Kamakura; a private company making swords exclusively for the navy (S).
xxi) Toyokawa Naval Arsenal (S).
xxii) Toyokawa Naval Arsenal (S).
xxiii) Tōkyō Gasu Denki KK (Tokyo Gas and Electric Co.).
xxiv) Tōkyō Explosives Factory.
xxv) 1st Tōkyō Arsenal (formed 1936).
xxvi) Heijō (Inchon) Ordnance Factory, Korea.
xxvii) Ōsaka.
xxviii) Chiyoda.
xxix) Tōkyō Branch Ordnance Depot, Toyokawa. Navy.
xxx) Yokosuka. Navy.
xxxi) Asashi Factories.
xxxii) Unidentified (S).
xxxiii) 2nd Tōkyō Arsenal (1936–45).
xxxiv) Kokura Arsenal control stamp (post-1929) (S).
xxxv) Department of Control (chief inspector, navy), Tōkyō.

ARSENAL, ACCEPTANCE AND TANG MARKS

Fig. 35 shows a number of stamps found on swords and bayonets. Most are true arsenal marks but the Seki stamp (xvi), as explained above, is an army acceptance stamp. It can be regarded as post-1942.

Fig. 36 illustrates stamps found on swords and dirks, some being extremely rare. The most common is the Shōwa stamp (i), a military acceptance stamp that does not relate to any particular arsenal or centre. It appears to have been superseded by production-centre stamps such as Seki after 1942. Both can be found on gendaitō.

When found on a signed blade, acceptance stamps are located above the signature though there are exceptions like the Matsu stamp (fig. 36 xii). Those below a signature are generally kakihan (personal seals) used only by master smiths. See figs 35 and 36.

Figs 35-8; plates 50, 97.

Fig. 36. Other marks found on naval dirks and shin and kai-guntō blade tangs:

i) Shōwa stamp. A post-1926 military (army) inspection or acceptance stamp, very common prior to 1941/42.

ii) The 'Five Measures' stamp – *go* (5) – *to* (measure of capacity, 1 tō = 3.97 imperial gallons). Significance unknown; very rare.

iii) Tan or Kitau stamp meaning 'to forge' or 'forged', and probably used to indicate a hand-forged blade. Scarce.

iv) Ma kane hisa stamp – literally 'true-metal-ancient', i.e., made from old steel. Rare.

v) Wa stamp, significance unknown. Rare.

vi) Na or mei stamp. Very small and easily overlooked, this is probably a general inspection or acceptance stamp – as well as a Nagoya Arsenal firearms control stamp. Fairly common.

vii) Dai or tai stamp, significance unknown. Very rare.

viii) Chimata stamp, significance unknown. Very rare, but can be confused with (i). Once found in conjunction with a 'Seki' stamp. It appears to date from the later part of the Second World War.

ix) Probably a naval inspection or acceptance stamp of the Taishō and Shōwa eras. (Found on a naval dirk crossguard.)

x) Unidentified (from a naval dirk crossguard).

xi) Hisa stamp, significance unknown. (Found on a naval dirk crossguard.)

xii) Matsu stamp, significance unknown. Very rare, it is apparently limited to blades (both signed and unsigned) found in late-1944 pattern shin-guntō mounts.

xiii) Kami (God) stamp, significance unknown. Very rare. Found only on a shin-guntō tsuba, it could be confused with (i).

Fig. 37. Examples of one- and two-character 'Kakihan' (a smith's personal seal) in a cartouche, occasionally found under tang signatures.

i) Kane-uji used by Kaneuji.
ii) Taka character used by Kanetaka.
iii) Kane-hisa used by Kanehisa.
iv) Zane character used by Kanezane.

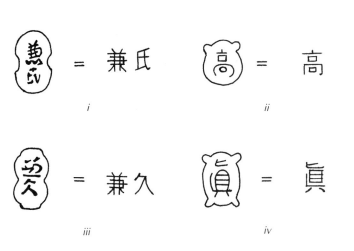

Fig. 38. Examples of stylised kakihan without a cartouche, used by:
i) Ishidō Mitsunobu.
ii) Hara Morinobu.
iii) Minamoto Moritaka.

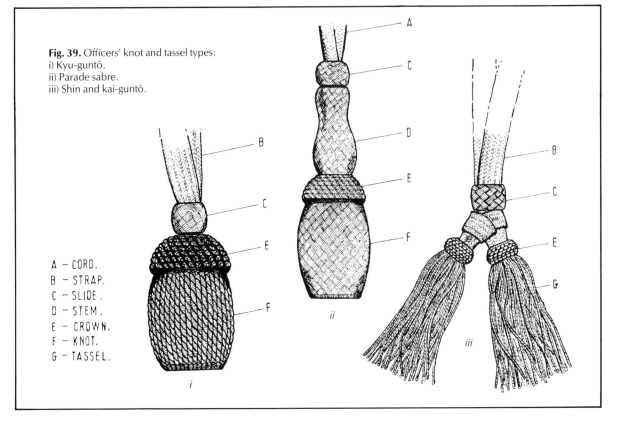

Fig. 39. Officers' knot and tassel types:
i) Kyu-guntō.
ii) Parade sabre.
iii) Shin and kai-guntō.

A – CORD.
B – STRAP.
C – SLIDE.
D – STEM.
E – CROWN.
F – KNOT.
G – TASSEL.

Sword knots and tassels

All military swords had knots or tassels (figs 39, 40), but early examples are unfortunately virtually non-existent. By necessity, uniform prints and contemporary photographs have been used as a guide.

Army and navy kyu-guntō swords surrendered in 1945 are often found with standard shin and kai-guntō tassels.

Surrender photographs indicate that not all swords were handed over with their tassels, which may have been removed by the Japanese officers to avoid a certain measure of disgrace.

ARMY

Army NCOs, c.1873. A bullion or leather strap with a slider and an elongated knot having zig-zag stitches. Colour unknown.

Cavalry Troopers. Probably a black or brown leather strap with a leather knot similar to the army NCOs' shin-guntō pattern.

Cavalry officers. A black cord with a solid knot and crown, similar to the officers' kyu-guntō pattern.

Army NCOs' kyu-guntō. Unknown, but thought to be similar to the NCOs' shin-guntō pattern.

Army officers' kyu-guntō. A black linen strap with a large solid black knot and crown (German-style). The knot has a gold bullion slider and a gold base. General officers may have had a black linen strap with gold knot in the same style. A light-coloured knot and cord (possibly gold) is shown in 1904–5 photographs of the Russo-Japanese War.

Army officers' parade sabre. A gold cord, slider and knot with stem. Between world wars, the army officers' kyu-guntō pattern appears to have been worn.

Army NCOs' shin-guntō. A ³⁄₈in wide brown leather strap with a slider. The barrel-shaped leather knot has longitudinal serrated strips.

Army officers' pattern shin-guntō. All have linen straps approximately ⁵⁄₁₆in wide (width and thickness varies), with sliders and tassels. The colour depends upon rank:

i) For company officers – brown with blue lining; brown and blue tassels.

ii) For field officers – brown with red lining; brown and red tassels.

iii) For general officers – brown with red lining, and yellow cotton or gold wire zig-zag stitches; yellow tassels.

iv) For civilian advisers to the army (Gunshoku) – officer equivalents as for company, field and general officers above dependent on rank; NCOs equivalents, plain brown linen straps and tassels. The Gunzoku, or Gunshoku, had ranks equivalent to the regular army, but a different rank indication. They were entitled to wear tassels with the appropriate colours on their swords. Officer equivalents wore olive green uniforms, while NCO equivalents wore khaki. (Information from the War History Department of the Japanese National Defense Agency, Tōkyō, and courtesy of Han Bing Siong.) Presumably, NCOs also carried the army officers' shin-guntō.

Army officers' late-1944-pattern shin-guntō – plain brown straps and tassels (presumably because uniform rank distinction had been abandoned on the battlefield).

Tassel variants
Known variations of shin-guntō style tassels include:

i) Maroon with blue lining; maroon and blue tassels.

ii) Maroon with red lining; maroon and red tassels.

iii) Green with blue lining; green and blue tassels.

iv) Green with yellow lining; green and yellow tassels.

These uncommon variants may be made from braid or a silk mixture, and have a different weave pattern from the regular shin-guntō versions. The straps can also be up to ¹⁄₂in wide.

Such tassels are often ascribed to officers of the army administration department but no evidence to support this can be found. The History Department of the Japanese Defense Agency, Tōkyō, confirms that these officers had ranks equivalent to the regular army and would have carried the same

Fig. 40. An army NCO leather knot.

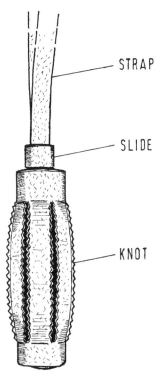

STRAP

SLIDE

KNOT

colour-patterns. Alternatively, it has been suggested that the tassels were substitutes for Japanese supplies in occupied areas but, again, the normal colour system would be expected. Perhaps the most plausible explanation is that they were worn by non-Japanese officers who served in volunteer units attached to the Japanese army. The colours may reflect the national flags, or alternatively form a ranking system.

Shin-guntō style tassels are currently available in the normal weave pattern with thicker straps having a padded feel. Colours are unusual (e.g., brown and yellow), probably intended for the present day Self-Defense Force.

NAVY

Naval kyu-guntō, c.1896. Full details remain unknown, but the four variants are all thought to be of gold bullion with gold cords:

i) For petty officers – an elongated stem with tassels.

ii) For superior petty officers – an elongated stem with an acorn knot.

iii) For commissioned officers – an elongated stem with a barrel knot.

iv) For flag officers – a crown with tassels or 'worms' (bullion ringlets).

Naval officers' kyu-guntō, c.1914. Plain gold cords, with a gold slider and knot displaying red vertical zig-zag stitches. The knot has a red base and is larger than the naval parade sabre knot. A black army kyu-guntō knot is also found, but its official sanction may be lacking.

Naval NCOs' pattern kai-guntō. Unknown; possibly the same as the officers' version.

Naval officers' pattern kai-guntō. The same as the army officers' shin-guntō type, but plain brown.

Naval officers' parade sabre. Plain gold cords. The gold slider, stem and knot have vertical red zig-zag stitches and the knot has a red base.

OTHERS

Diplomats. A wide woven gold-bullion strap, stem and tassel.

Meiji-period police sword. Probably the same as the army NCOs' shin-guntō.

Police parade sabre. Probably the same as the army NCOs' shin-guntō.

METHODS OF TYING

Kyu-guntō knots of all periods are looped through the knucklebow-slot and wrapped around the guard until a short or medium length section hangs down.

Shin-guntō tassels which denote rank are looped through the saru-te as shown in fig. 43 and then tied around the hilt for service wear in the manner illustrated in fig. 44. In the case of the 1944 pattern shin-guntō, with no saru-te, the straps are stitched together after one section only has been passed through the kabuto-gane (fig. 41 iii). One tassel must be bound tight and pulled through to achieve this.

All shin-guntō pattern knots have the straps tied together in a special way above the tassels (fig. 42).

Figs 39-44.

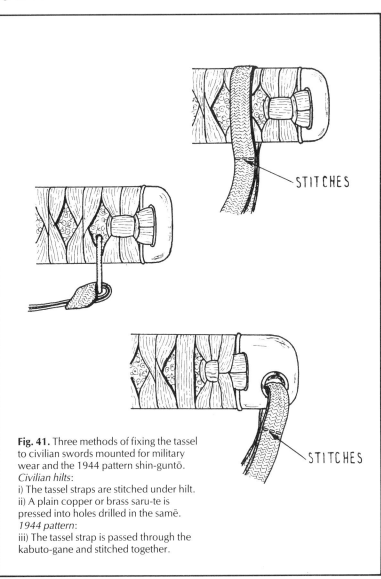

Fig. 41. Three methods of fixing the tassel to civilian swords mounted for military wear and the 1944 pattern shin-guntō. *Civilian hilts*:
i) The tassel straps are stitched under hilt.
ii) A plain copper or brass saru-te is pressed into holes drilled in the same. *1944 pattern*:
iii) The tassel strap is passed through the kabuto-gane and stitched together.

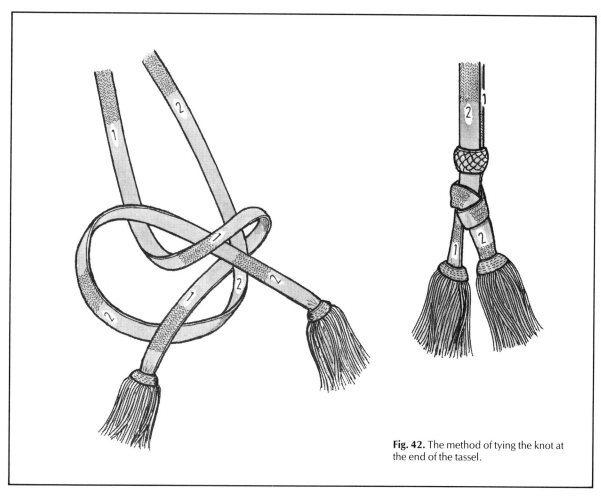

Fig. 42. The method of tying the knot at the end of the tassel.

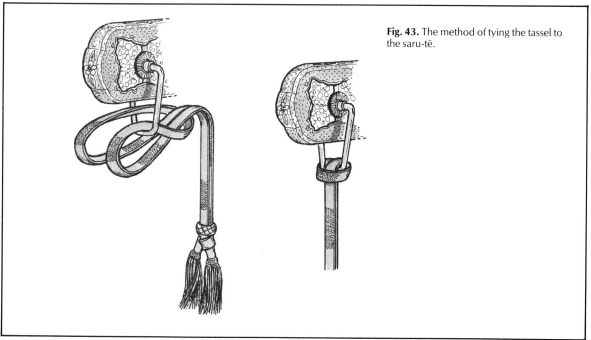

Fig. 43. The method of tying the tassel to the saru-tē.

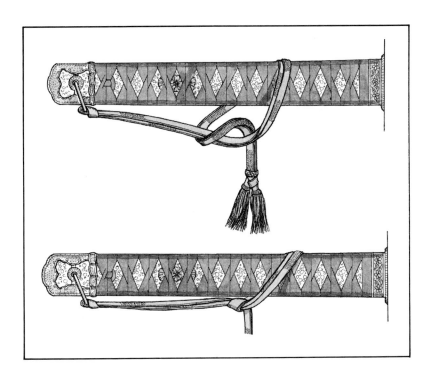

Fig. 44. The method of tying the tassel round the hilt for service wear.

Fig. 45. A Meiji period black leather frog (see plate 2).

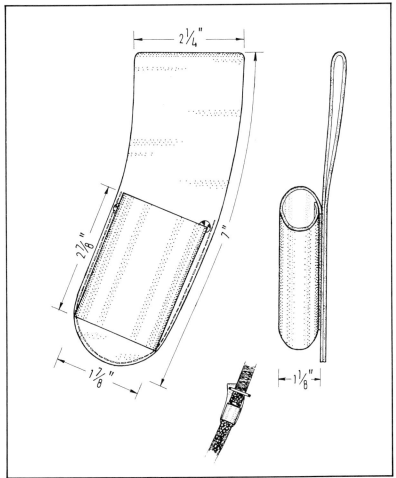

87

Sword belts

Sword belts are rare, especially those made before the Shōwa period; however, slings or hangers are sometimes found with swords. The most commonly encountered hangers are from army service belts of the Second World War and may be plain leather, interwoven leather or steel linked chains.

Black leather naval service belts of all periods followed the British pattern.

All belts had a brass or steel hook attached to either the belt or upper sling so that the sword could be hung in the regain position (almost vertical) while leaving the carrier's hands free.

In common with the sword knots, many of the following patterns have been deduced from coloured prints or contemporary photographs. The lists may be incomplete and additions or corrections will be welcomed.

Army belts

Sword pattern	Belt	Clasp
Katana and wakizashi, 1868–71	A leather(?) frog suspended from the shoulder or waist belt (fig. 45).	Unknown.
1871 and 1873 officers' pattern	The service belt of black or brown leather has two slings. (Similar to fig. 46.)	Two-piece, circular. Motif unknown.
1873 NCOs' pattern	As above.	A single claw, with a rectangular steel buckle.
1873 pattern officers' dress sword	A V-shaped velvet or leather(?) frog, suspended from a coloured belt. General – a red belt facing? Lieutenant- and major-general – a gold bullion belt facing with three stripes (red?).	Circular, gilt brass; motif unknown.
Diplomatic corps dress sword	A V-shaped black velvet frog suspended from a white watered-silk shoulder belt.	None.
Cavalry troopers' sabre	A 1¾in wide brown leather belt with one adjustable sling (fig. 46).	A single claw, with a rectangular steel buckle.
Kyu-guntō	A field service belt of brown leather, with one sling (or two?).	As above.
Officers' shin-guntō	A field service belt of 3in wide green or khaki canvas, with a brown leather tongue; one sling.	Two claws, with a rectangular steel buckle.
Officers' shin-guntō (and possibly kyu-guntō)	A 1⅛in wide dress belt of black leather, with one sling (or perhaps two?). It is lined internally with felt coloured according to rank. Field officers (and generals?) – red. Company officers – blue.	A two-piece circular gilt-brass clasp with rays radiating from a central sun (fig. 47 i).
NCOs' shin-guntō	A field service belt of 2½in wide brown leather; one sling.	Two claws, with a rectangular steel buckle.

Unidentified	A brown leather belt, with its two slings faced with gold bullion and a central narrow black stripe.	A single claw, with a rectangular steel buckle.
Unidentified	A black leather belt, its two slings faced with gold bullion, a central silver stripe and narrow red edge stripes.	S-shaped silver or steel.

Note

Shin-guntō, when carried in the field, were sometimes slung diagonally across the back by means of an adjustable leather belt. This left both hands free.

Figs 45-7, 50; plates 2, 34, 102-6.

Fig. 46. A sword hanger, possibly for cavalry, used in the Russo-Japanese war and probably as late as the First World War. The belt is leather with a solid brass slider and a ¾in-wide leather hanging strap. The fittings comprise a brass regain-hook with a steel buckle and clip.

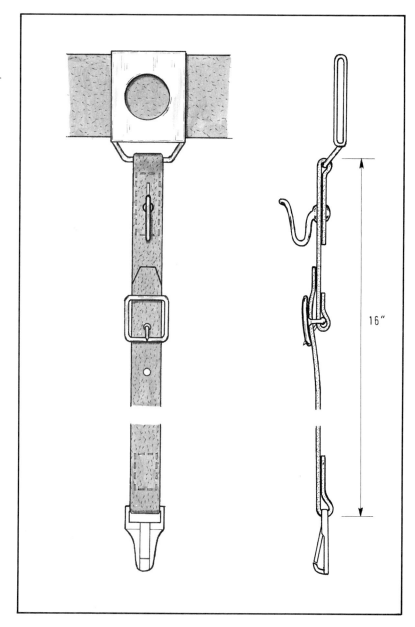

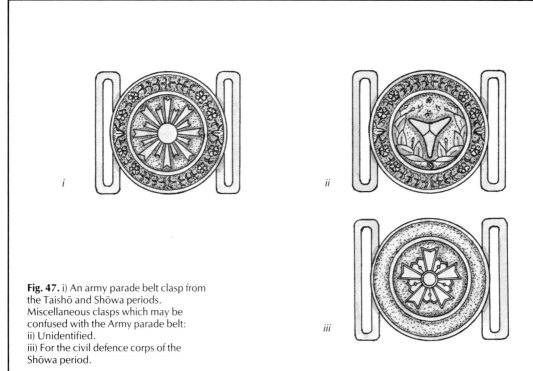

Fig. 47. i) An army parade belt clasp from the Taishō and Shōwa periods. Miscellaneous clasps which may be confused with the Army parade belt:
ii) Unidentified.
iii) For the civil defence corps of the Shōwa period.

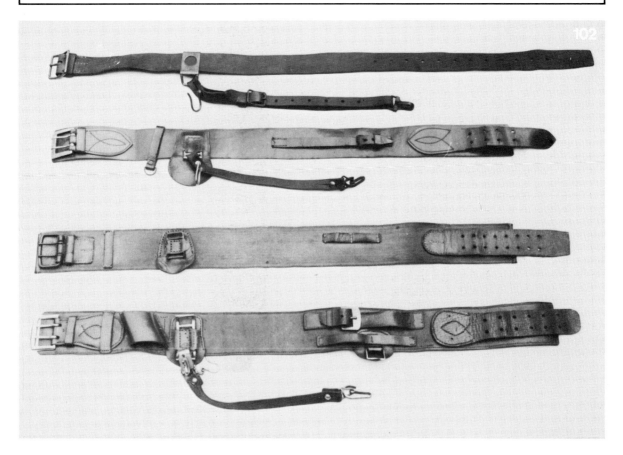

103

Plate 102. Army sword belts for service wear.
Top to bottom:
i) A cavalry trooper's for sword pattern of c.1886.
ii) A sergeant-major's Shōwa-period brown leather belt.
iii) An officer's green canvas belt from the Second World War.
iv) An officer's brown leather belt of the Shōwa period.
(R. Gregory collection.)

Plate 103. The army officers' brown leather service belt, showing probable use of the loop that is sometimes encountered. Such a method of carrying prevented the sword from rattling and left both hands free. (R. Gregory collection.)

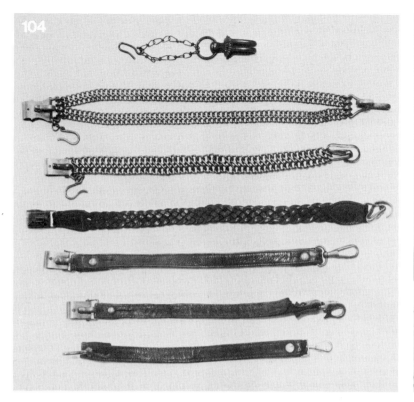

Plate 104. Army sword hangers – three metal and four leather – for use with service belts. The uppermost is non-standard, but appears original, while the lowest is black leather with a black felt lining and a small brass spring clip. This may be naval, since army leather service hangers are normally brown. (R. Gregory collection.)

Plate 105. An army cadet in parade uniform, with dress sword belt and shin-guntō sword; c.1939.

Plate 106. An army officers' parade belt with a hanger. The black patent-leather belt has a brass buckle, and is lined internally with coloured felt denoting rank (blue for company officers; red for field or general officers). It belongs to the Taishō or Shōwa periods. (R. Gregory collection.)

Naval belts

Sword pattern	Belt	Clasp
Wilkinson 1872 pattern	An admiral's dress belt, with two slings, heavily embroidered with gold bullion laurel leaves.	The circular gilt-brass clasp has a central foul anchor with the rope entwined with the cross-stay only. The two crossed stems with sakura are set over the vertical stay (fig. 48).

Unidentified, probably Meiji-period	A 1½in wide black leather belt with two slings.	The circular gilt-brass clasp has a chrysanthemum (kiku) blossom above a foul anchor (fig. 49 vi).
Officers' kyu-guntō, c.1896	A black leather service belt with two slings.	The circular gilt-brass clasp has a central motif according to rank (fig. 49 i-iv).
Officers' kyu-guntō, c.1896	A dress belt with two slings decorated to match.	As above, with a central raised silver motif.
a) Flag officer	A horizontal gold bullion facing with narrow black edge stripes.	A Paulownia imperialis (kiri) with seven central flowers and five on each side (fig. 49 i).
b) Flag officer (reserve)	A diagonal gold bullion facing with narrow black edge stripes.	As above.
c) Senior officer	A gold bullion facing with narrow black central and edge stripes.	An anchor, and a Paulownia imperialis (kiri) with five central flowers and three on each side (fig. 49 ii).
d) Senior Medical officer	A gold bullion facing with narrow black central and red edge stripes.	As above.
e) Junior officer	Black outer stripes and one gold bullion inner one of equal width.	A foul anchor with a sakura blossom in centre (fig. 49 iii).
f) Petty officer	A black patent leather belt.	A foul anchor (fig. 49 iv).
Officers' kyu-guntō, c.1914, and kai-guntō, c.1933	A black patent leather service belt with two slings. The dress belt facings were the same as those of the pattern of c.1896 (see above).	The centre of the circular gilt-brass clasp has a foul anchor and sakura for all officer ranks. (The silver motif was discontinued.) (Fig. 49 v.)
Kai-guntō (naval land-warfare or garrison units)	A 2½in wide brown leather service belt, with two slings.	The rectangular steel buckle has two claws (although there are three lines of holes).
Marines and gunners, c.1873	Unknown.	The circular gilt-brass clasp displays the motto NIPPON KAI HO HEI TAI (Japanese gunnery units and marines) outside an inner design that probably varied according to rank (fig. 49 vii).

Figs 48-9; plate 107.

Fig. 48. An 1872 pattern belt clasp designed by the Wilkinson Sword Company for the Imperial Japanese Navy.

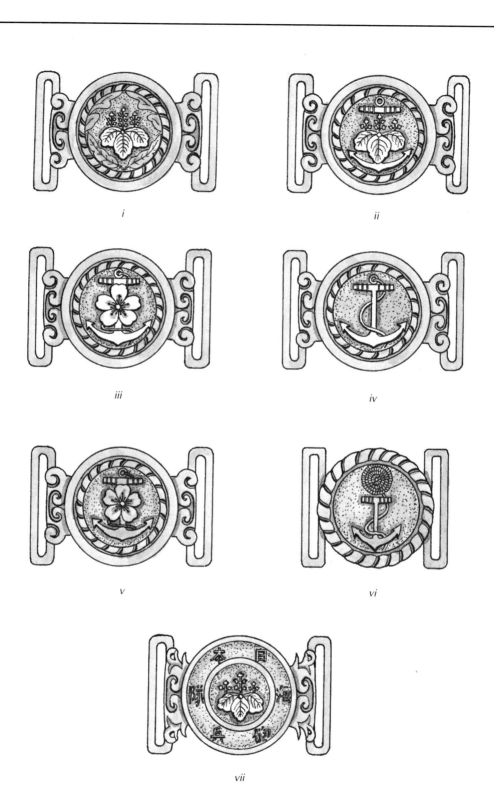

i

ii

iii

iv

v

vi

vii

Fig. 49. Some naval belt clasps: These Meiji-period examples from *c*.1896 are gilded brass with raised silver central motifs:
i) Flag officers.
ii) Senior officers.
iii) Junior officers.
iv) Petty officers.
v) Belt clasp for all commissioned officers, *c*.1914. Used in the Taishō and Shōwa periods. Made of gilded brass, it superseded the four Meiji patterns shown above.
vi) An unidentified clasp, possibly used by commissioned officers prior to 1896.
vii) A clasp for marines and gunnery commissioned officers, *c*.1873. This example may be for a flag officer.

Fig. 50. Detail of a scabbard (saya) in forward-pointing service wear, showing the leather suspension strap looped under and clipped to the ashi (ring), which has been hooked over the brass regain-hook.

Plate 107. Naval officers' black leather service belts. *Top*: Taishō or Shōwa-period. See fig. 49 v. *Bottom*: unidentified. Possibly pre-1896; see fig. 49 vi. (R. Gregory collection.)

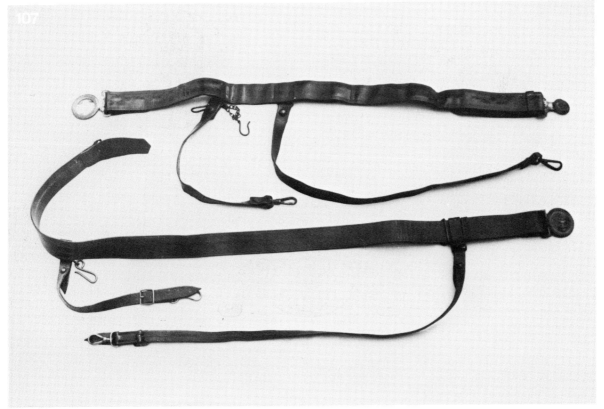

The Mon

A 'mon' is a Japanese family crest, or perhaps more accurately called a badge. Originally deriving from about 350 basic designs, they proliferated to over 7,500. They are formed from natural objects (though rarely animals), geometric shapes, Japanese calligraphy and inaminate objects.

Mon are hereditary, being handed down the male line with variations that are sometimes subtle. Important families could have two or three badges; the most important (requiring registration) is the 'jo-mon', while those for everyday use are termed 'kaye-mon'. Different families often shared the same mon. They form a study in their own right.

An officer could – if he wished – have his mon affixed to the hilt of his sword, usually in the form of a ⅜-½in diameter silver disc. They are fixed by a rear pin, split pin or solder on the pommel, backstrap, fuchi or menuki. They can be found on army and naval kyu-guntō, shin and kai-guntō and parade sabres, but not on police sabres. This is probably because the military services tended to attract those from ex-samurai and better-class families.

At the surrender in 1945 many officers deliberately defaced or removed their mon, to avoid disgracing the family name.

Figs 51 and 52 illustrate typical mon. All have been copied from examples found on military swords. See also plate 108.

Plate 108. A silver mon on the kabuto-gane (pommel) of a shin-guntō. This is the most common location. This mon of three oak leaves (kashi) is shared by the Makino, Horimoto and Kasai families among others. (R. Gregory collection.)

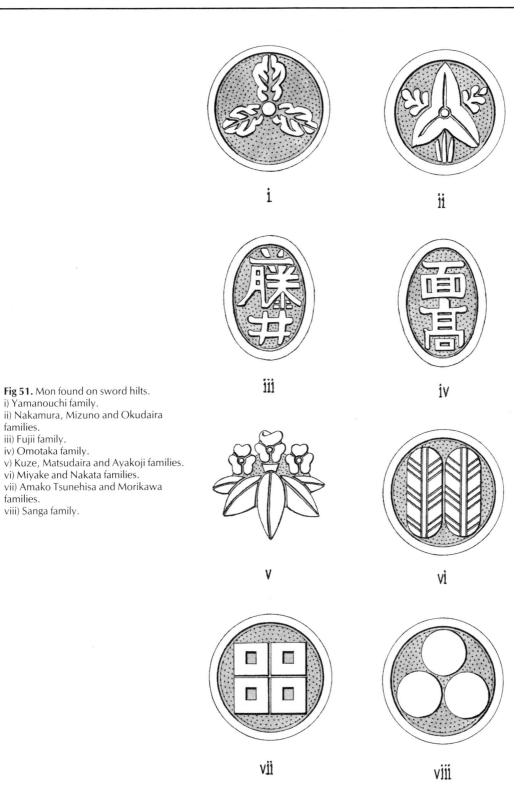

Fig 51. Mon found on sword hilts.
i) Yamanouchi family.
ii) Nakamura, Mizuno and Okudaira families.
iii) Fujii family.
iv) Omotaka family.
v) Kuze, Matsudaira and Ayakoji families.
vi) Miyake and Nakata families.
vii) Amako Tsunehisa and Morikawa families.
viii) Sanga family.

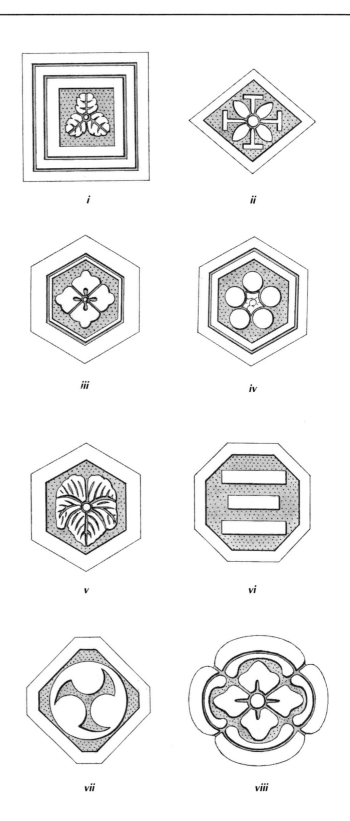

Fig 52. Mon found on sword hilts.
i) Kasai family.
ii) Possibly a branch of the Nakagawa family.
iii) Possibly a branch of the Oda family.
iv) Kaga family.
v) Takatora family.
vi) Sadamichi and Masanari families.
vii) Kuribayashi family.
viii) Asakura and several other families.

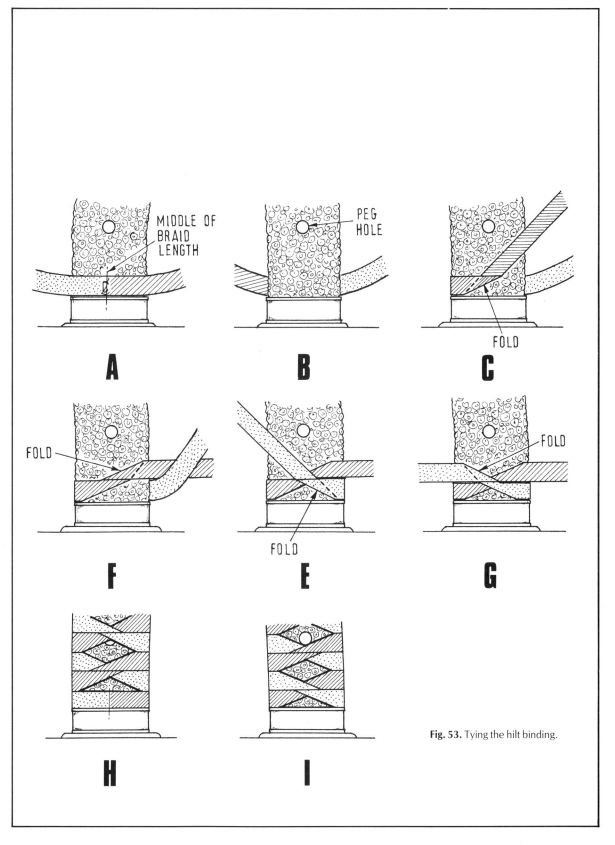

Fig. 53. Tying the hilt binding.

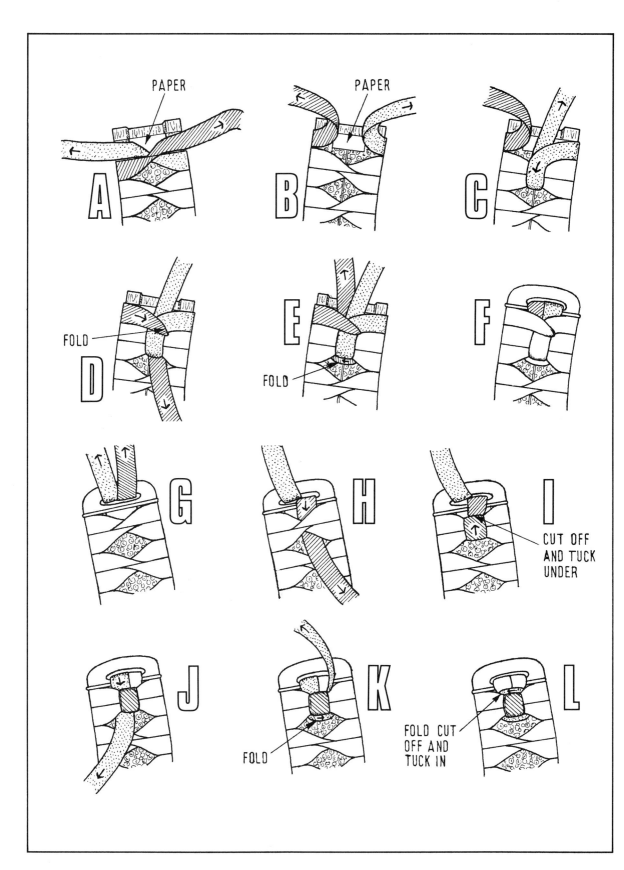

Sword surrenders

Fig. 54. A method of tying the hilt binding at the pommel (kashira).

The bulk of Japanese military swords now seen in the west arrived after the Japanese surrender on 2 September 1945.

A million or more military swords were carried by Japanese officers and NCOs during the war years in China, Manchuria, the Pacific area and other areas of Japanese penetration. In fact, some officers owned two or three.

Lord Mountbatten insisted that all surrendering officers must hand over their swords at properly constituted ceremonies. Senior officers presented their swords to the British or Commonwealth officer presiding, while the junior officers filed out and laid theirs on the ground. They were collected and distributed as trophies, the surplus being destroyed. Many surrender ceremonies did not occur until 1946, because the British used fully-armed Japanese to quell rebellions by nationalist and communist dissidents. The Japanese were also allowed to police certain areas where Allied troops were not available. Disarming was not ordered until repatriation could be organized.

US forces under General MacArthur implemented similar surrenders, but most swords were obtained in Japan after the occupation. They were collected and issued as souvenirs to US military and naval personnel who served in the South West Pacific. The Japanese were forbidden to possess old civilian swords, and thousands were confiscated for distribution or destruction. An official US estimate of swords and sabres obtained shows that 661,621 were captured and surrendered; 372,609 were dispersed as trophies, or for museum and technical use, and 289,012 were destroyed. None returned to Japan.

The number of Japanese swords obtained in the British (SEAC), Australian, Chinese and Russian theatres is unknown, but must have been immense. 11,000 swords were reportedly collected in Thailand alone.

The intrinsic value of Japanese military swords is clearly demonstrated by the following letters, from Japanese officers who were finally ordered to surrender their swords after working with British officers in Sumatra and Malaya. Letters of this type are rare and of great interest to the collector.

Swords with ancestral and Shōwa-period blades were regarded with equal esteem. Reluctance to surrender a symbol of authority and a most valued possession is apparent, throughout the letters.

Plates 109-16.

NB. In the letters describing the sword-surrenders, no attempt has been made to correct the spelling and grammar of the originals, thus preserving their 'period quality' and charm.

SURRENDERED TO LT. COL. R. C. W. THOMAS IN FRENCH INDO CHINA 24 DEC 1945 BY LT. COL. MIYAHARA, HQ JAPANESE ARMY

Colonel D.S.C. Rossier
Commander Sub-Area Padang
ALF Sumatra

Sir,

Being informed that you have been appointed Commander Sub-Area Padang, I have a pleasure to present you here this sword of mine, and express hearty congratulations for your promotion of rank and position.

The sword I am presenting to you bears the name KANEMOTO, most famously called SEKI NO MAGOROKU which is well authorized by the historians of Japanese swords. This sword was made approximately 350 years ago, and is classified as the later 'old sword'. KANEMOTO is the name of the maker of this sword, and he lived in 'Mino', or the present 'Gifu' prefecture, in central or the most mountainous region in Japan, as one of the most famous sword-makers of that age. It was an age just at the end of long and destructive days of war and conflict.

The shape of this sword is an even bow-curve, and shows a good deal of lustre. The pretty edge-waves are generally called the 'sanbon sugi' (or a variation of three cryptomerias), and they are comparatively narrow in shape. The sanbon sugi is a noteable feature of this sword. And an 'old sword' in general, we say reminds us of the dark blue firmament at night of profound peace and silence. I hope that you would appreciate the gracefulness and at the same time severity of the Japanese Samurai spirit seen through the sword. To my regret, however, the scabbard of this sword is more or less delapidated, mostly due to the days of operations as a regiment commander at the Indian and Burmese fronts, but it will by no means lessen the value of the sword itself.

I, the Commanding Officer of the Japanese 25th Independent Brigade, representing the whole Japanese forces in Central Sumatra, wish to send you a word of sincere goodwill, and expect as ever your fair considerations towards the coming various matters concerning our army.

Sincerely yours,

(signed)

Kimio Omoto, Major-General
Officer Commanding Japanese
25th Independent Mixed Brigade

Padang, Sumatra,
25th March 1946.

This sword is now in the Royal Lincolnshire Regiment Museum.

Japanese Central Contact Bureau
Padang 20 May 1946

Captain J. D. Drabble
GSO HQ Padang Sub Area.

Sir,

Now leaving Padang very soon, I consider a great honour to be able to hand you my sword personally.

This sword I am presenting is not an old sword, it is a SHŌWATŌ by name, which means that it was made in the Era of SHŌWA on July 1942. The name of the maker is MASATSUNE and I believe he is still living in Japan. The wave on the blade is the special trimmer of this sword. I have brought this sword all the way through this with love and respect.

Finally in handing over this sword, I wish you a happy future with Health and Good Luck.

(signed)

(SAKAE OGATA 2nd/Lt)
Interpreter and Liaison Officer
Japanese Central Contact Bureau

This sword is now in the Royal Lincolnshire Regiment Museum.

Plate 109. This surrender plaque, which reads 'Sorrendered to Lt.Col. R. C. W. Thomas in French Indo China 24 Dec 1945 by Lt.Col. Miyahara H.Q. Japanese Army', was obviously engraved locally – note the spelling mistake! Lieutenant-Colonel Miyahara was chief staff officer to HQ Traffic Facilities at the headquarters of the Southern Army, Saigon. (R. Gregory collection.)

Plate 110. This well-engraved surrender inscription appears on the habaki of an army officer's shin-guntō. The obverse reads 'Surrendered by Shosa [Major] Nagamura Kiyotaka, Japanese VIII army, Emirau Island, 21st March 1944'. The reverse reads 'To A. B. Boyles, U.S.M.C.'. This is an example of a spurious postwar engraving added to increase value: research indicates that Emirau was evacuated by the Japanese two months *before* the invasion of the US 4th Marines on 20 March 1944. The USMC has no record of an A. B. Boyles. (R. Gregory collection.)

Japanese Central Contact Bureau.
Padang. 15th April 1946.

To: Officer Allied Land Forces
   PADANG.   SUMATRA.

NIPPON-TŌ The Japanese SAMURAI SWORD

The swords we are handing over to you here are ones that formerly belonged to the ablest officers in our 25th Independent Brigade. Most of them were made about 250 to 300 years ago in districts where our famous sword-makers lived. They are all precious ones and some of them are those that the great old Japanese feudal lords possessed for themselves, and duly deserve to be a national treasure. For example, the MAGOROKU, the MUTSU-NO-KANESADA, OSAFUNE-NO-SUKESADA, KUNINORI, BIZEN-NO-KUNIMATSU, etc.

From the old Japanese SAMURAI (at present age Japanese Soldiers especially characterised in officers) has respected their swords as their spirits, and it was common for them to make promises 'in the name of their swords', which means they will commit 'Harakiri' suicide, and die together with his sword, his spirit if he should break the promise. They love it and respect it most deeply and solemnly, and make it a rule to keep it always within the reach of their hand. We can well imagine how deep their sorrow was when they at last had to part with them with which their ancestors went to war, and with which they themselves had been together all the way through this long war. But nevertheless, since the sword and its owner is traditionally and spiritually one, even though it may happen to part temporarily with his master will safely return to him again in the long run, it is believed.

I, as Chief Negotiator with Allied Officer in Central Sumatra Area, representing all the owners of these forty swords expect from the bottom of my heart that these SAMURAI SWORDS will always be loved and respected by you, their new masters, on behalf of Japanese Officers, their former owners. It needs to be an expert to appreciate the swords properly, but it is a good thing to try to see the mysterious solemnity, its long history and the authentic and technical meaning it bears in itself. We can well say here that the NIPPON-TŌ is one of the first and foremost symbol of the Japanese soldier's spirit.

In reliance, entrusting everything to your high virtue and gentlemanship.

Yours sincerely,

(signed)

(SHIGEMI OHNO, Captain.)
Officer Commanding.
Japanese Central Contract Bureau.

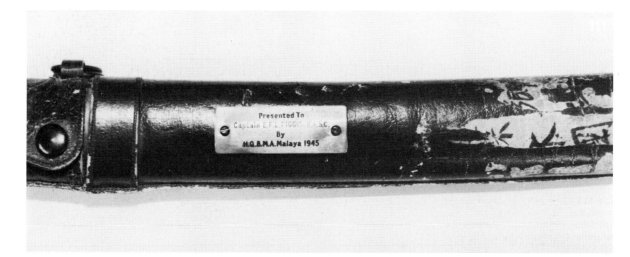

Plate 111. A typical presentation plaque, reading 'Presented to Captain E. F. L. FIGGIS. R.A.S.C. [Royal Army Service Corps] By H.Q.B.M.A. [Headquarters British Military Administration] Malaya 1945'. The remains of a paper label name the former Japanese owner as Umeki Kunitaro. (R. Fuller collection.)

Plate 112. 31 of the swords surrendered at Tampoi, Johore State, Malaya, by officers of the 7th Army Headquarters on 25 February 1946. (IWM photograph SE 6857.)

Plate 113. Army officers surrendering swords at Kuala Lumpur, Malaya, September 1945. Note the plaited and plain leather hanging straps. (IWM photograph IND 4846.)

Officer Commanding,   Central Contact Bureau.
Field Security Section,   Padang, SUMATRA.
ALF. Padang.   18th April 1946.

Sir,

Being informed that you are going to be promoted to a new and higher position very soon; I hereby have the pleasure to present you this sword of mine in hearty congratulations, and in recognition of our meeting in Padang.

This sword I am sending you here bears the name GASHŪ NO JU KANEWAKA which means made by KANEWAKA of GASHŪ DISTRICT. Gashū is the present ISHIKAWA PREFECTURE and is in the NORTH WEST of Central Japan which is a cold district and which is noted from old for producing great sword makers, together with the Central Districts proper. KANEWAKA was a famous sword maker born in this district and later well authorised by historians of Japanese Swords. This sword was made approximately 250 years ago, and is classified as an early NEW SWORD (swords made earlier than 350 years ago is classified as old SWORDS). It was the age of new feudal peace of the Tokugawa era.

The shape of the sword (the blade) is rather wide in width and slightly heavier than the ordinary old sword and does not shine too brightly, but it cuts deep and well. The shape of the wave in the blade, tempering, is what we call TEIJI shape (⌐_⌐_⌐_⌐) which is neither regular nor irregular zig-zag, nor a straight line as seen in most common swords. This sword needs a little polishing by an expert to make it reveal its real beauty, owing to my rather rough use during this war, but you can plainly see the characteristics of the wave in the lamp light very clearly. I hope you would be able to recognise its extreme severity and at the same time the special gracefulness of the old Japanese SAMURAI spirit, which is expressed wholely in the sword.

I cannot help heaving a deep sigh of sorrow in parting with my most beloved sword, my spirit, with which my ancestors went to war and which my father himself handed over to me when I set out from home for this war, praying for my heroic victory in every action. But now as we are finally going to be obliged to entrust everything to you, it is my great pleasure that this sword can be presented to you with whom I have worked together to this day with interest and respect, and be kept safely in your hands.

I, as Commanding Officer, Japanese Central Contact Bureau, Sumatra, wish to send you a word of sincere goodwill, and pray for your safe voyage and your ever good luck.

                                      Yours sincerely,

                                      (Shigemi Ohno, Captain)
                                      Officer Commanding
                                      Japanese Central Contract Bureau,
                                      PADANG.

                                    Johore Bahru, 8th June, 1946.

Brigadier M.S.K. Maunsell DSO OBE,
Commander, British Inter-Service Mission
            to French Indo-China.

Sir,

I have the honour of presenting to you, in fulfilment of my promise of last year, my treasured Japanese sword, which I have cherished during all my campaigns in 1937–45, and which by your sufferance I have retained to date.

An excellent specimen of the eighteenth century Japanese sword-smiths' art, it is not unworthy, I believe, of presentation to a true representative of British Army, who by his high-minded conduct and truly chivalrous actions has commanded my highest respect and admiration during the months of our context in French Indo-China. I am very glad to bequeath my treasured possession to so gallant a gentleman as your good self.

With the kindest personal regard, I remain,   Faithfully yours,

                                      (signed)
                                      Takazo Numata, Lieut.-General.

Plate 114. Captain Tsuneki IJN, 12th Naval Guard Force commander, surrenders his kai-guntō to Captain Murphy RN at Mergui in Burma, 19 October 1945. This unique ceremony was the only naval surrender to have occurred in Burma. (R. Gregory collection.)

Plate 115. Captain Chiyoji Tsuneki IJN walking back after surrendering his sword (see Plate 74). Note the naval land-garrison pattern service belt. (R. Gregory collection.)

◁ Numata was Chief-of-Staff to the Southern Army at Saigon. He remained in office until June 1946, co-ordinating the evacuation of Japanese personnel in south-east Asia with Brigadier Maunsell. He also surrendered a sword to Lieutenant-General Frederick Browning at Singapore in September 1945 who returned it to Numata in September 1952 – a very rare occurrence indeed.

This sword is in shin-guntō mounts and has an unsigned blade attributed to the Sukenaga school of Bizen province, mid-18th century. It is now in the Gregory collection.

APPENDIX 1 JAPANESE MILITARY SWORDS – COMPARATIVE DIMENSIONS

All the dimensions in this section have been taken from swords examined by the authors. However, as so many variations are encountered, these figures should only be taken as a guide.

a) Overall length measured while the sword was in the scabbard, from the pommel cap to the chape or shoe drag base.
b) Hilt length measured from inside the guard (tsuba) to the pommel top.
c) Scabbard length measured from the throat to the base of the chape or shoe.
d) Blade length measured along the back-edge from the tip to the hilt, on mass-produced sabres, or to the machi (back notch) of traditional-style blades – i.e., the habaki length is not included. Where the sword possesses a traditional-style blade and a fixed hilt (such as that of naval non-commissioned officers), the length includes the habaki.
e) Blade width measured at the widest part of the blade.
f) Tang length measured from the tang tip to the back notch of traditional-style blades.

	LENGTH			BLADE			WEIGHT		DESCRIPTION
	Overall length IN	Hilt length IN	Scabbard length IN	length IN	width IN	Tang length IN	Sword and scabbard OZ	sword OZ	
REBELLION KATANA, 1877	40½	9	29½	27	1	7	40	30	Unsigned blade. Iron mounts. Black-lacquered scabbard.
REBELLION WAKIZASHI, 1877	23⁷⁄₁₆	5¹³⁄₁₆	17⁷⁄₁₆	16¹⁄₁₆	1⅛	4	24	19½	Unsigned blade. Iron mounts. Signed tsuba. Black-lacquered scabbard.
UNIDENTIFIED SWORD TYPE I	30½	6⅜	24¼	23	1	4½	36	26	Unsigned kotō blade (pre 1596). Hand-engraved brass mounts. Chromium-plated scabbard. Black samē grip.
UNIDENTIFIED SWORD TYPE II	36⅜	8½	28	21	1	5½	38	28	Black leather-covered scabbard. Plain brass mounts. Black samē grip. Unsigned blade.
DIPLOMATS' SWORD	31¼	5⅞	25½	22	½	hilt fixed	22	16	Etched blade. Gilded mounts. Black leather scabbard with wood base.
1886 ARMY CAVALRY TROOPERS' SABRE	36⁵⁄₁₆	5	31⁵⁄₁₆	30¼	1	hilt fixed	45	28	Mass-produced blade. Steel mounts and scabbard. Note weight difference.
	36¾	5	31½	30½	1	hilt fixed	54	32	
ARMY OFFICERS' KYU-GUNTŌ	37½	8	29¼	25½	1¹⁄₁₆	5	53	38	Blade signed SUYEKUNI *c.*1450. Gilded mounts. Chromium-plated scabbard.
	41½	10¾	30½	25	1	4½	64	44	Blade signed SEKI (NO) JU KANEKUNI. Possibly Meiji or Taishō. Gilded mounts. Chromium-plated scabbard.
CIVILIAN WAKIZASHI	27	5½	21	18½	1	5	30	18	Cut-down hand-forged blade. Civilian mounts. Leather-covered civilian lacquered scabbard.
ARMY OFFICERS' SHIN-GUNTŌ	33⅝	8⅞	24½	19	1¹⁄₁₆	5	38	30	Blade signed KUNIYUKI. Possibly Shintō (1596–1867).
	37	9½	27½	24¾	¹⁵⁄₁₆	5¼	52	33	Blade signed BIZEN (NO) KUNI (NO) JU TADAMITSU, *c.*1500. Steel scabbard.

	LENGTH			BLADE			WEIGHT		DESCRIPTION
	Overall length	Hilt length	Scabbard length	length	width	Tang length	Sword and scabbard	sword	
	IN	IN	IN	IN	IN	IN	OZ	OZ	
	39 1/8	10 1/16	29 1/16	22 15/16	1 3/16	8 1/2	44	33	Shōwa blade signed SAKAMUKI KANESHIGE. Leather-covered civilian black-lacquered scabbard.
	39 3/8	10 1/8	29 1/8	25 1/4	1 3/16	8 1/2	59	39	Blade signed KANEMUNE, showā. Steel scabbard.
	40 1/4	9 1/2	30 3/8	27 3/8	1	7 1/2	54	37	Blade signed KUNIKANE, *c.*1600. Civilian mounts and iron tsuba. Leather-covered field scabbard.
	40 9/16	10 3/16	29 1/2	26 3/16	1 7/32	8 3/8	59	39	Blade signed KANENORI, 1943. Steel scabbard.
LATE 1944-PATTERN ARMY OFFICERS' SHIN-GUNTŌ	38 7/8	10 1/4	28 1/2	26 3/16	1 1/4	9	60	38	Blade signed YOSHITADA, 1945. Iron mounts. Steel scabbard.
	39 1/4	10	28 3/4	26 3/4	1 1/16	8	55	42	Blade signed MUNETOSHI, 1942. Iron mounts. Brown-lacquered wooden scabbard.
	39 3/8	10 1/4	28 3/4	25 3/4	1 1/8	8	61	40	Blade signed KANENOBU, 1943. Iron mounts. Black-lacquered wooden scabbard.
ARMY NCOs' SHIN-GUNTŌ	38	8 5/8	29	26 1/2	1 3/32	8 1/4	60	38	Numbered blade. All-metal hilt and scabbard. The dimensions of three other examples agreed to within 1/8″ overall and 1/2oz in weight.
ARMY NCOs' SHIN-GUNTŌ (EMERGENCY ISSUE)	37 5/8	10 1/8	27 1/2	23 9/16	1 1/8	7 3/4	54	44	Officers' pattern arsenal blade. All-metal hilt. Iron tsuba. Leather-covered black-lacquered scabbard.
ARMY ERSATZ SHIN-GUNTŌ	39 3/16	9 1/4	29 5/16	26 11/16	1 1/4	7 11/16	56	41	Arsenal blade. Leather field scabbard. Red tape bound hilt.
ARMY 'HOME DEFENCE' SHIN-GUNTŌ	40	10 3/8	29 1/2	26 3/4	1 1/4	9	63	44	Unsigned blade. All-steel mounts and scabbard.
ARMY OFFICERS' PARADE SABRE	36	5 1/4	30 3/4	29 1/16	15/16	fixed hilt	32	16	All have plated blades, gilded mounts, horn grips and chromium-plated scabbards.
	37 1/2	4 7/8	32 1/4	31	13/16	fixed hilt	32	19	
	39 3/4	5 3/8	34 1/8	32 1/4	13/16	fixed hilt	32 1/4	20	
NAVAL OFFICERS' KYU-GUNTŌ, *c.*1874	36 3/4	5 1/4	31	30	1	3	40	28	Gilded mounts. Black leather scabbard.
NAVAL OFFICERS' KYU-GUNTŌ	39 5/8	9 1/2	30	27 1/8	1 1/8	5 1/2	56	41	Blade signed SUKESADA, 1579. Gilded mounts. Black shagreen scabbard.
NAVAL OFFICERS' KAI-GUNTŌ	38 13/16	9 3/4	28 3/4	26 7/16	1 5/16	8 5/16	53	42	Shōwa blade signed TSUKUSHI MASAMITSU SAKU. Gilded mounts. Shagreen scabbard.
	38 3/8	10 3/16	27 7/8	26	1 1/4	8 3/8	52	39	Shōwa blade signed NŌSHŪ SEKI (NO) JU MURAYAMA YOSHITSUGU SAKU. Gilded mounts. Samē scabbard.
NAVAL NCOs' KAI-GUNTŌ	39 1/2	11 1/2	28	26 3/8	1 3/16	fixed hilt	43	34	Arsenal blade. Plain brass mounts. Black leather-covered wooden scabbard.
NAVAL OFFICERS' PARADE SABRE	32 11/16	5 1/8	27 9/16	25 1/16	3/4	fixed hilt	25	17 1/2	Plated blade. Gilded mounts. Shagreen scabbard.
	32 11/16	5 1/8	27 13/16	26	3/4	fixed hilt	25	18	Plated blade. Gilded mounts. Leather-covered scabbard.

	LENGTH			BLADE			WEIGHT		DESCRIPTION
	Overall length	Hilt length	Scabbard length	length	width	Tang length	Sword and scabbard	sword	
	IN	IN	IN	IN	IN	IN	OZ	OZ	
NAVAL DIRKS	14¾	4	10¼	8¾	⅝	2¼	10	7	Arsenal blade. Gilded mounts. Shagreen scabbard.
	14¾	4	10½	8¾	⅝	2½	10	7	Grooved blade. Gilded mounts. Samē-covered scabbard.
	16⅝	4	12¼	8¾	⅝	2½	11	7	Grooved blade. Gilded mounts. Samē-covered scabbard.
ARMY CAVALRY OFFICERS' SWORD	34⅜	6	28	24	1	4¾	44	28	Unsigned blade. Gilded mounts. Samē-covered hilt.
POLICE SABRE	24½	5	19⅜	18	¹³/₁₆	hilt fixed	28	19	Plated blade, gilded mounts and chromium-plated scabbard.
KAMIKAZE DIRKS	10⅜	3⅝	6⅞	6¼	¾	1¾	7	4	Leather-covered hilt and scabbard with suspension cords. Ivory hilt.
	9¼	3¼	6⅛	5⅜	¾	1½	5	3½	Dark rosewood hilt and scabbard. Covered as above.

SEKI SWORDSMITH SOURCE LINE

1229: MOTOSHIGE
1259: KANENAGA
1272: second-generation KANENAGA
1571: eighth-generation KANETSUNA
1396: 168 houses of Seki-based smiths.
1600: 90 houses.
1836: 68 houses.
1870: sword-wearing ban.
1876: sword-owning ban.

From the time of the sword ban, the swordmakers became cutlers, blacksmiths and machine workers. Worried about losing swordsmiths from Seki altogether, Kaneyoshi made a small number of swords in this period. After his death in 1914, as many of Kaneyoshi's ideas as possible were implemented by his pupil Watanabe Kanenaga in the latter's Japanese sword school. The Seki masters include Kaneyoshi and Kanenaga (both deceased), Kojima Kanemichi (alive, 2 pupils) and Asano Kanezane (alive, 3 pupils). Twelve Seki swordsmiths currently exist.

Plate 116. A collector's nightmare. Typical of the fate of hundreds of thousands of swords at the end of the Second World War, these are being shovelled into a furnace in Japan. (Private photo collection.)

The authors wish to express their thanks to James Silver, and to George Trotter of Australia who provided the translation.

All Japanese swordsmiths took a pride in their work, even those of the Shōwa period working through the war years. This is touchingly demonstrated by quoting from a letter received by an American collector, James Silver, who had tried to trace the maker of a gendaitō sword in his collection.

In 1975 he located the smith, Asano Kanezane of Seki, who, at the age of 65, was running a foundry in Seki – making kitchen knives and flat irons under the name of Shinichi Asano. The letter from the Seki Board of Education said:

'In his Golden Age, he got many prizes in the All-Japan sword contest … When he saw the rubbing of the sword (tang) he was very surprised and realised the sword was really the thing he made. Especially the stamp under the name was proof of his own (work). He wondered, why and how you got it. He asked to tell you "Please take care and keep it forever" . . .'.

Kanezane's blades are good quality gendaitō and have either Shōwa (pre-1942) or Seki (post-1942) acceptance stamps. His blades also have his personal seal (fig. 37 ii) under the signature. See also Oshigata appendix in this book. The fact that he produced them during the war years was still so sensitive that he had tried to forget his previous achievements.

A further enquiry in 1982 succeeded in obtaining a reply from Kanezane himself, which is reproduced below in its entirety. This unique and fascinating document includes his family and personal history, a rare insight into the sword industry of Japan by a man who took part. It is also proof that Seki was not an 'arsenal' and that gendaitō were made there.

The following brief personal history and history of Seki was supplied by Kanezane:

19 December 1910.	Born Asano Shinichi.
April 1917, age 8.	Entered primary school.
March 1923, age 13.	Graduated from primary school.
April 1923, age 13.	Apprenticed to Kojima Kanemichi.
April 1930, age 21.	Became independent and received art name KANEZANE from his teacher.
1930 onwards.	Worked as swordsmith in Seki, his birthplace.
April 1931, age 22.	Took his first pupil, Kanetada, age 13.
April 1933, age 24.	Took his second pupil, Michizane, age 13.
April 1934, age 25.	Took his third pupil, Kanemasa, age 13.
1934, age 25.	Entered the Fine Art Exhibition for the first time, winning the silver award.
1935 onwards.	Entered the Fine Art Exhibition for the second time; winning the gold award.
1936–41.	Won the gold award in each annual Fine Art Exhibition.
1942, age 33.	Received the Special Award at the last Fine Art Exhibition.

KANEZANE'S LETTER TO J. SILVER, LOS ANGELES, USA

Greetings in reply,

Thank you for your letter. I can only say how I am thankful for the kind words regarding the sword I made. If I look back, I'm not sure just how many swords I made, but I put my heart and strength into every one of them. That some of them have been protected and cherished in a far country is a thing that gives me a joyful feeling. Well, about myself. At the age of 13 years I was apprenticed and finished after a period of seven years, becoming independent at 20 years. From around 23 years of age I took an apprentice and together we strove wholeheartedly in study, until, by 25 years of age I had taken 3 apprentices with whom I expended every effort daily. When one is making art objects one has a different feeling than usual, and when making such objects I prayed to the Kami (God) for assistance, and with the aid and encouragement and sympathy of my three apprentices we concentrated wholly on these objects. Such work cannot be done alone, only with sympathy of my pupils could we see the completion of these art objects. I won an award in the Fine Art Exhibition, after that I participated annually in the exhibition. In the spring of 1942 I received the Special Award. This was the final exhibition.

In the old days, modern machinery was non-existent, therefore one used one's self strenuously. If one thinks about it now it was really a fantastic thing. Around 1934 onwards the craftsman of Seki became swordsmiths and Seki became an active town where they made and sold swords. Soon World War Two became intense; in 1942 we came under the management of the Army Sword Co. At the back of my house was established the East Asia Sword Co. with more than 80 employees. Here the manufacture of Guntō proceeded earnestly. In Seki a lot of sword companies were established. After the end of the war we changed over to peaceful cutlery companies and by manufacturing kitchen knives, etc., all of us just managed to survive. After the end of the war, all of the closed Seki sword companies assiduously promoted the cutlery business which caused postwar Seki to become famous in relation to other cutlery producing towns. In these last 10 years there have been occasional markets (for swords) in Seki.

In 1952 I closed my peacetime cutlery company, after that my own house by cutlery and other things came to support a living*. In recent times, by machine, my eldest son and myself, the two of us make meat slicers, steak knives, kitchen knives, etc., out of Swedish steel. Although I am now 73 years of age, my years of expertise in this area (metalwork) could be helping me, and even now I can work in this field.

I couldn't imagine that the swordsmith's craft which I love would end in such a short 10 years†. It was the flower of my life that ended at the end of the war. When I look back now it was my very fragile dream. I think it was around 1960 that Japanese swords returned to be treated as art objects, but I had changed to peaceful manufacturing at the end of the war, and I made up my mind that I will never return to sword making. I thought swordsmithing was only for the war. Now I am old and cannot do it alone, but looking at swords brings back melancholy memories from the past. Sometimes when I become melancholy I talk to my wife about those times when I was devoted to making swords with my apprentices.

Because I have no education, I spent my life in my work without trying to write anything, this letter is disjointed and I am sorry for this. Also I apologise for the delay in replying to your letter.

Sincerely,

(signed)

Asano Shinichi (Kanezane)

*A small family business, run from the home, is typical Japanese practice.
†He must mean the period 1934–45 when he was fully committed to swordmaking.

COLLECTING

Before buying, the collector is advised to take certain precautions. The following are only general hints.

● Ascertain the sword pattern is as described. Auction houses often describe army parade sabres as police swords or naval kai-guntō as naval kyu-guntō. Perhaps obtain a reference to this book for clarity.

● Check shin- and kai-guntō for showatō blades by looking for the blunted cutting edge adjacent to the habaki.

● Check that the hilt securing hole matches that on the tang if the peg is missing, using a matchstick or holding the sword up to the light if necessary. If the holes do not match, the blade has been switched.

● Count the number of peg holes on a tang if it is a Shōwa blade. More than two holes could mean that the blade has been switched. A new hole drilled to line up with that in the hilt may be artificially aged.

● Check all tang signatures before buying if possible. The claim 'it is a signed blade' may only reveal a signature that reads 'made in the Tōkyō no. 1 ordnance workshop'.

● The condition of the blade is a matter for the individual. Red stains are rust: not blood, as is sometimes claimed. Even the smallest fault or stress mark can devalue a good blade.

● Check the fittings. Tsuba should be correct for method of retaining the sword in the scabbard, e.g., a push-fit type should not have a slot for spring-clip retention. Similarly, a push-button spring clip is not found with a field scabbard unless a metal throat is provided with a suitable slot.

● Compare the blade length against the scabbard length. An old wakizashi blade (i.e., short) may be found in a longer military scabbard. Shōwa blades should match to within about four inches. The blades should also fit fairly tightly in the scabbard, although wood liner shrinkage and wear occurs.

● Beware undocumented claims that, for example, a sword comes from the Imperial Guards: military swords have no divisional or regimental marks.

● Ensure the blade and scabbard numbers match on NCOs' and cavalry troopers' swords.

● Linen surrender or transportation tags with Japanese calligraphy often contain the owner's name, rank and unit. As they can easily be exchanged, it is a buyer's risk when accepting any claim about origin.

● Hilt fittings should be fairly tight, though the wood base does shrink over the years and allows some movement. An old tsuba may have been removed and replaced by a military example – so check wear marks and that the correct grading of seppa is used.

The following blade-tang inscriptions show some of the many variations which may be found with military sword mounts. They include unique and rare items such as that made for a Japanese general, an inscription added to an old blade during the Second World War, and a cutting test (tameshigiri) on a human body. Others are more common, typifying those more frequently encountered on machine-made and gendaitō (hand-forged) blades.

Oshigata: tang rubbings

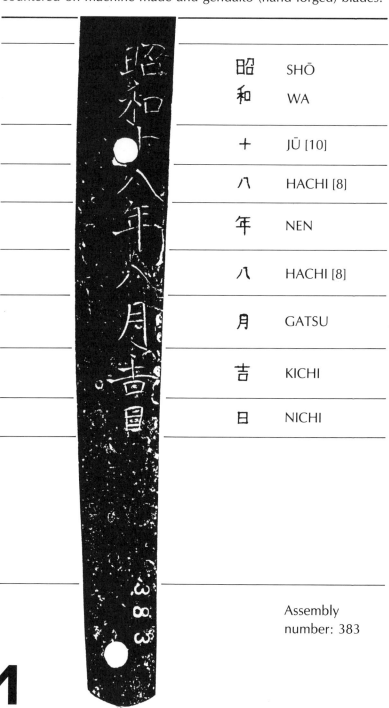

昭	SHŌ
和	WA
十	JŪ [10]
八	HACHI [8]
年	NEN
八	HACHI [8]
月	GATSU
吉	KICHI
日	NICHI

Assembly number: 383

1

KATSUNOBU [of the] Tōkyō Number 1 Army Ordnance workshop. Star stamp. A lucky day, August 1943.

DAI = number. RIKU = land. GUN = military. ZO = worked or made. HEI = war. SHŌ = workshop.

A gendaitō in shin-guntō mounts.

	STAR STAMP	
	TŌ-	東
	KYŌ	京
	DAI	第
	ICHI [1]	一
Army	RIKU-	陸
	GUN	軍
Ordnance workshop or Arsenal	ZO-	造
	HEI-	兵
	SHŌ	廠
	KATSU-	勝
	NOBU	信

1

3

SHŌ-WA	昭和
JŪ [10]	十
SHICHI [7]	七
NEN	年
JŪ [10]	十
ICHI [1]	一
GATSU	月
KICHI	吉
NICHI	日

1

刃	HA-MI	味
最	SAI-JŌ	上

2

中	NAKA-YAMA
山	
博	HIRO-MICHI
道	
試	TAMESU
之	KORE WO

Column 1. HAMI (literally 'taste of cutting edge', i.e., quality of sharpness), SAIJŌ (the best, the highest) – 'The highest (or best) quality cutting ability'.

Column 2. NAKAYAMA HIROMICHI, TAMESU (tested), KORE WO (this) – 'Nakayama Hiromichi tested this'.

Column 3. SHŌWA JŪ SHICHI NEN JŪ ICHI GATSU KICHI NICHI – 'A lucky day, November 1942'.

Column 4. NI OJITE (in accordance) TAKEHARA SHŌGUN (general) MOTOME (request of) NI OITE (for) SHOBU (military councillor or minister of state) DAIKA (his honour) – 'Made in accordance to the request of his Excellency, Military Councillor, General Takehara'.

Column 5. KURIHARA AKIHIDE SAKU KORE WO – 'Kurihara Akihide made this'.

Chu-kissaki. Ko-maru boshi. Komidare hamon with nioi and some nie. Faint but indeterminate hada. Shin-guntō mounts with general officers' tassel.

Smith

Kurihara Hiko Saburō Akihide, who died in 1954, was a gendaitō smith and student of second generation Inagaki Shoo. He originally came from Tochigi prefecture near Tōkyō. An active politician, he opened an academy for sword study in Akasaka, Tōkyō. Among his students were gendai smiths Akimoto, Akitomo and Miyairi Yukihiro.

Owner

General Takehara, for whom this blade was made, is almost certainly Lieutenant General Saburō Takehara. He may have been an adviser or head of a military academy at the time the blade was made, owing to the title used.

What little of his personal history can be assembled from a variety of sources is as follows: major-general, October 1939; commander of Infantry Division Kumamoto (6th Division), April 1941; 1942–1944, unknown; lieutenant-general; commanded 49th Division from its activation in Korea, January 1944; this division transferred to Burma in July 1944, where it fought until the cessation of hostilities; Takehara personally surrendered to Major-General Crowther, 17th Indian Division commander, at Thaton, Burma, in the last week of October 1945. Although he surrendered a shin-guntō at this time, senior officers often had two or more swords and it cannot be guaranteed that the 'surrender sword' was the one described here.

Tester

The tester is master swordsman Nakayama Hakudo, sometimes called Hiromichi. (1869–1958), the sixteenth headmaster of the Jinsuke Eishin line of Shimomura-Ha sword discipline. He popularized the term 'Iai-Do'. The test was carried out on a straw bundle or green bamboo, simulating a body.

It is extremely rare for an officer's rank to be engraved on a tang, as is a Shōwa-period tameshigiri (blade testing) inscription. This is also a rare example: a general's sword, authenticated by the blade inscription. Since it is inscribed in the same hand as the smith's signature, there can be no question of postwar engraving.

(R. Gregory collection)

4	
NI OITE	於
SHŌ-BU	相武
DAI-KA.	台下

4	
NI OJITE	應
TAKE-HARA	竹原
SHŌ GUN	將軍
MOTOME	需

5	
KURI-HARA	栗原
AKI-HIDE	昭秀
SAKU	作
KORE WO	之

2

117

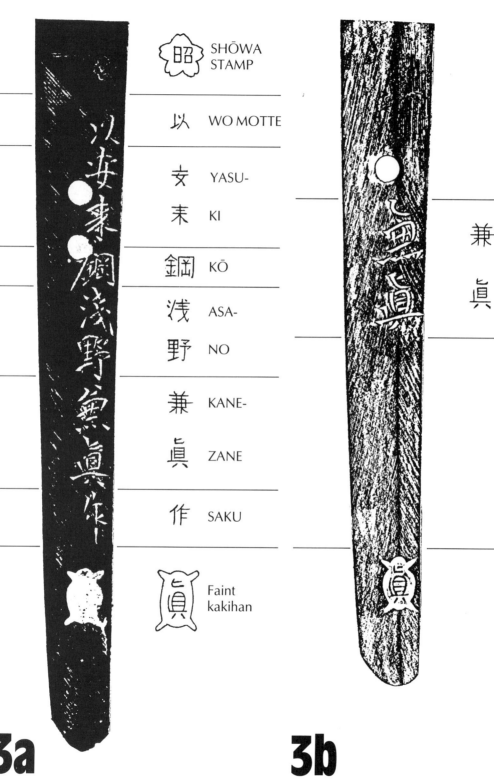

3a

昭	SHŌWA STAMP
以	WO MOTTE
安	YASU-
支	KI
鋼	KŌ
浅	ASA-
野	NO
兼	KANE-
眞	ZANE
作	SAKU
眞	Faint kakihan

3b

	Faint SHŌWA STAMP
兼	KANE-
眞	ZANE
	Kakihan (smith's personal seal)

3

A. WO MOTTE YASUKI KŌ ASANO KANEZANE
SAKU – 'Made by Asano Kanezane using
Yasuki steel'. Shōwa stamp (pre-1942).

B. KANEZANE. Shōwa stamp (pre-1942).
Suguha hamon of fine konie. Tight
mokume hada. 26½in blade; ¹¹⁄₁₆in sori.
Shōwa-period civilian mounts.

Compare the signature style of B with the
more common A. Kanezane, a good
gendaitō smith of Seki, won several gold
awards from 1935 to 1942. Formerly
known as Asano Shinichi, b.1910, he was
still alive in 1982.

A. *H. Gopstein collection.*
B. *G. Moody collection.*

4

MASAHIRO. SHŌWA NI JŪ NEN NI GATSU:
February 1945. Note the unidentified
stamp of CHIMATA character (i.e., forking
road, street, scene, arena, theatre). The
significance in this usage is unknown,
however. It has only been seen once
before on a similarly dated blade by
SHIGEKATSU – inferring that it is a late-war
stamp. This blade is in a late 1944-pattern
shin-guntō mounts.

L. Skorupa collection.

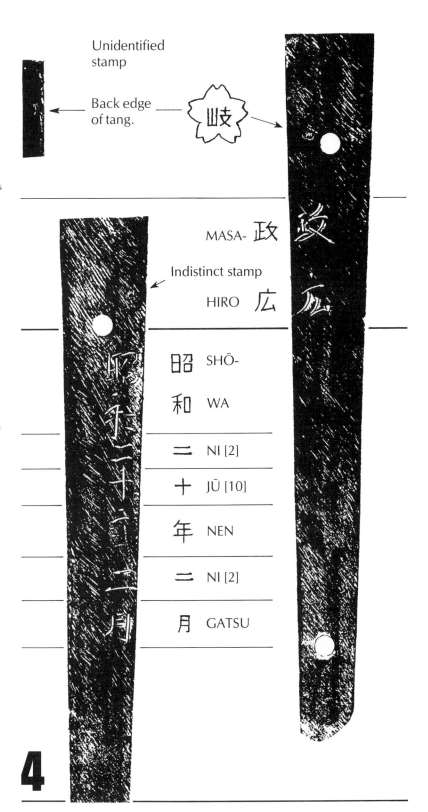

Unidentified
stamp

Back edge ——— 岐
of tang.

MASA- 政

Indistinct stamp

HIRO 広

昭 SHŌ-

和 WA

二 NI [2]

十 JŪ [10]

年 NEN

二 NI [2]

月 GATSU

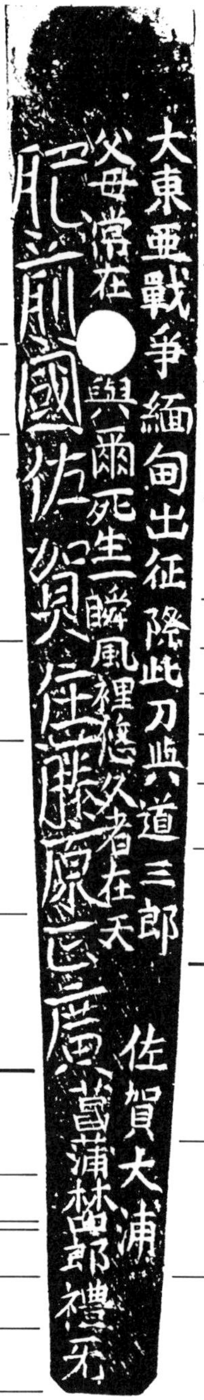

1

HI-ZEN	肥前
(NO) KUNI	國
SA-GA	佐賀
(NO) JU	住
FUJI-WARA	藤原
MASA-HIRO	正廣

菖	SHŌ-	蒲	BU
林	HAYASHI		
四	SHI-	郎	RŌ
禮	REI		
无	MU		

2

大東亜戰争	DAI-TŌ-A-SEN-SŌ
緬甸	BIRUMA
出征	SHU-SEI
際	SAI
此刀	KONO TŌ
與	ATAE
道	MICHI
三郎	SA-BURŌ
佐賀	SA-GA
大浦	Ō-URA

3

FU-BO	父母
TOKO	常
ZAI	在
ATAE	與
SHIKA	爾
SHI	死
SEI	生
ICHI	一
SHUN	瞬
KAZE	風
UCHI NI	裡
YŪ	悠
KYŪ	久
SHA	者
ZAI	在
TEN	天

5

This is a rare example of a later inscription – dating from the Second World War – being added to a much earlier blade, probably a family heirloom, for presentation purposes.

Column 1. HIZEN (NO) KUNI SAGA (NO) JU FUJIWARA MASAHIRO – 'Fujiwara Masahiro, living in Saga in Hizen province'.

This signature and date should make this the first-generation Masahiro, son of Yoshinobu (吉信). On the 27th day of the 4th month of the Kanei era (i.e., 30 May 1628), he was awarded the title of KAWACHI (NO) DAIJO – which one would expect to see used in 1637. He died in 1665.

The following inscription was done during the Second World War. English phraseology is difficult but, hopefully, gives the gist of the intended meaning.

Column 2. DAITŌA (Great East Asia) SENSŌ (war) BIRUMA (Burma) SHUSEI (departure for the front) SAI (occasion) KONO (this) TŌ (sword) ATAE (give, gift) MICHI SABURŌ – 'This sword is given to Michi Saburō, on the occasion of his departure to the Burma front during the Great East Asia war'.

Column 3. FUBO (parents) TOKO (ever, endless) ZAI (country) ATAE (give, gift) SHIKA (so, in that way) SHI (death) SEI (birth) ICHI-SHUN (a short time) KAZE (wind) UCHI-NI (in) YŪKYŪ (eternity) SHA (person) ZAITEN (heavenly, in heaven) – 'A gift (from your) parents to always (remind you) of your country. Birth to death is but a short time; (afterwards) the wind (will carry) you to eternal paradise'.

Column 4. SAGA ŌURA – 'Ōura in Saga' (presumably the family residence).

Column 5. SHŌBU HAYASHI SHIRŌ REI (ceremony, salutes, thanks) MU (not, is not, without) – 'Hayashi Shirō of Shōbu without ceremony'(?). The significance of this is not clear; it may be the name of the engraver.

On the reverse of the tang: KANEI JŪ SHI NEN HACHI GATSU KICHI NICHI – 'A lucky day, 8th month, 14th year of the Kanei era', (i.e., 1637).

寛	KAN-
永	EI
十	JŪ [10]
四	SHI [4]
年	NEN
八	HACHI [8]
月	GATSU
吉	KICHI
日	NICHI

5

P. Yorke collection.

SŌKA KANETOSHI of Nōshū (province) forged this. The Tan stamp indicates a hand-forged blade.

鍛 (stamp)		TAN STAMP
濃	NŌ-	
州	SHŪ	
拱	SŌ-	
加	KA	
兼	KANE-	
利	TOSHI	
鍛	KITAU	
之	KORE WO	

6

122

SHIYAWAKA SUMARA – '(made at) Sumaran (on) the island of Java'. It is unusual for a inscription to be entirely in katakana script, indicative of non-Japanese words.

SHIYAWAKA = Java island; SUMARAN = a garrison town in central Java, with a steelworks making swords for Japanese and presumably collaborating Indonesian officers. A rare and unusual inscription.

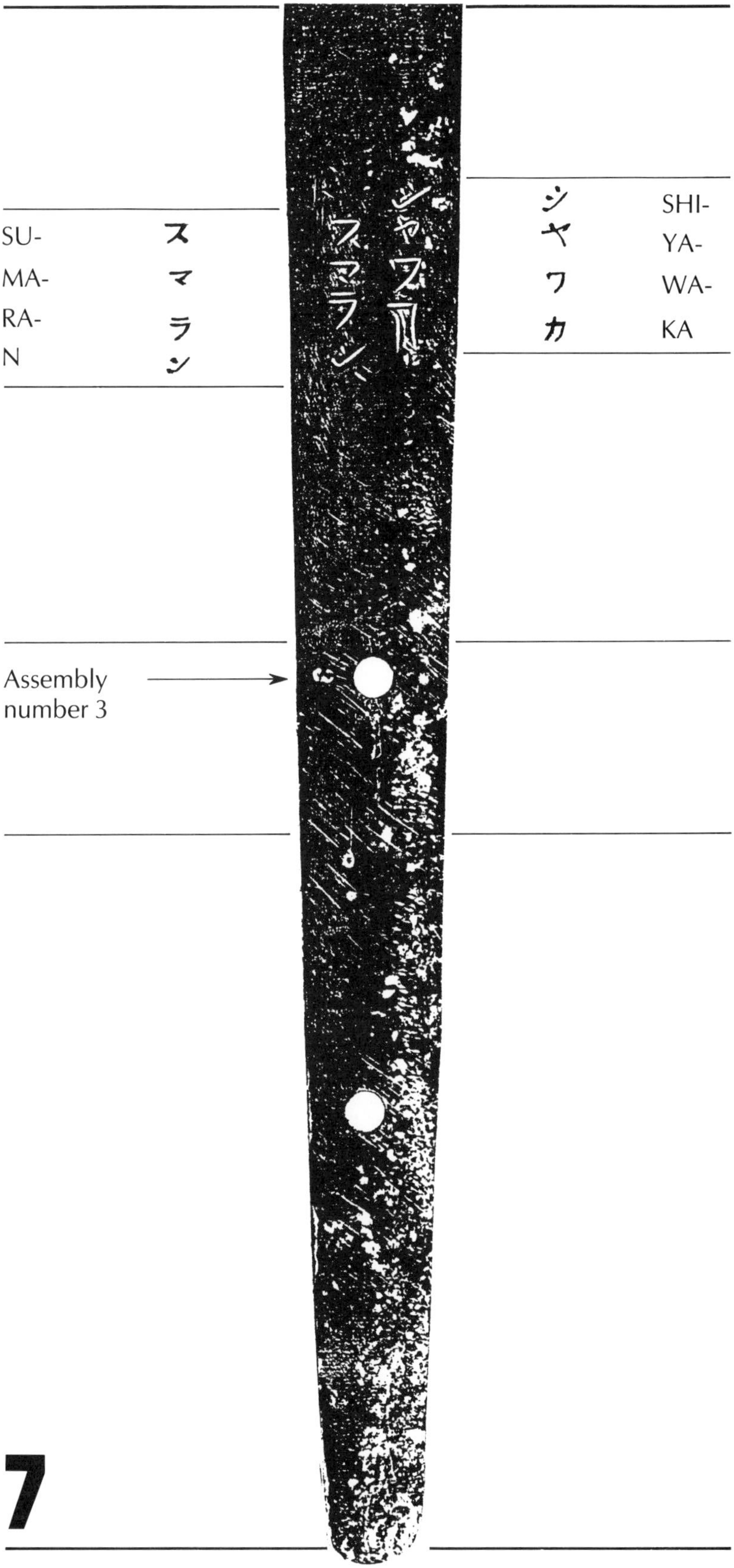

SU-MA-RA-N	スマラン	ジャウフマラン	シヤワカ	SHI-YA-WA-KA

Assembly number 3 →

7

2	
NI OITE	於
SEN-JU	千住
FUTA-TSU	二ツ
DO	胴
DO-DAN	土壇
FUTSU	拂

3	
NAGA-SAKA	長坂
MINAMOTO	源
TA-RŌ	太郎
TAMESU	試
KORE WO	之

1	
文久	BUN-KYŪ
二	NI [2]
年	NEN
三	SAN [3]
月	GATSU
十	JŪ [10]
八	HACHI [8]
日	NICHI

This blade was subjected to a tameshigiri (cutting test) on a human corpse.

Column 1. BUNKYŪ NI NEN (year) SAN GATSU (month) JŪ HACHI NICHI (day) – 'The 18th day of the 3rd month in the 2nd year of the Bunkyu era', i.e., 1862 (the date this blade was tested).

Column 2. NI OITE (at) SENJU (a suburb of Yedō) FUTATSU (2nd) DO (trunk) DO (earth, ground)-DAN (stage, dais) FUTSU (wield a sword) – 'At Senju, by the 2nd trunk cut and into the earth (or sand) mound'.

Column 3. NAGASAKA MINAMOTO TARO TAMESU (tested) KORE WO (this) – 'Nagasaka Minamoto (no) Taro tested this'.

Column 4. BUNGO (NO) JU (living in) TOMOYUKI – 'Tomoyuki, living in Bungo (province)'. There were a number of Bungo smiths of this name.

Ko-mokume jihada. Large choji-midare hamon. Chu-kissaki, Chu-maru. 27.4in blade. 0.7in curve (sori). Shin-guntō mounts with silver mon of standing water plantain (Mizuno family).

4

豊	BUN-
後	GO
住	(NO) JU
友	TOMO-
行	YUKI

8

Courtesy of R. Robertshaw

Bibliography

Die Japanische Armee in Ihrer Gegenwartigen Uniformierung. Leipzig, c.1910; German text.

The Russo–Japanese War Fully Illustrated. Kinkodo Publishing Co., Tokyo, 1904–5.

Bergamini, David: *Japan's Imperial Conspiracy.* Heinemann, London, 1972.

Dilley, Roy: *Japanese Army Uniforms and Equipment 1939–1945.* Profile Publications, London, 1970.

Fuller, R., and Gregory, R.: *A Guide to Showa Swordsmiths.* Privately published, 1978.

Fuller, R., and Gregory, R.: *Swordsmiths of Japan, 1926–1945.* Privately published, 1983.

Fuller, R., and Gregory, R.: *The Oshigata Book* (fully translated Japanese tang inscriptions of all periods). Privately published, 1985.

Gregory, R.: *Japanese Military Swords.* Privately published, 1971.

Hawley, William M.: *Japanese Crest Design* (chart of mon). Privately published, 1971.

Hawley, William M.: *Japanese Swordsmiths.* Privately published in two volumes, 1967; superseded by a combined volume, 1982

Honeycutt, F. L., Jr, and Anthony, F. Patt: *Military Rifles of Japan.* Julin Books, 1977 and 1983.

Manchester, William: *American Caesar: Douglas MacArthur 1880–1964.* Michael Joseph, London, 1982.

May, Commander W. E., and Annis, P. G. W.: *Swords for Sea Service.* Published in two volumes; HMSO, London, 1970.

Meeking, Charles (Ed.): *Pictorial History of Australia at War,* volume 5. Published by the Australian War Memorial, Canberra.

Meyer, S. L. (Ed.): *The Japanese War Machine.* Bison Books, London, 1976.

Rosie, George: *The War in Vietnam, 1956–66.* 1970.

Saburo Hayashi (in collaboration with Alvin D. Coox): *Kogun: The Japanese Army in the Pacific War.* 1959; reprinted, Greenwood, 1978.

Sasama Yuzankaku: *Nippon-no-Gunso*. In two volumes. Tokyo, 1970.

Tadao Nakata: *Imperial Japanese Army and Naval Uniforms 1869–1945*. Japanese text; English supplement. Arms & Armour Press, London, 1975.

Terraine, John: *The Life and Times of Lord Mountbatten.* London 1968; revised edition 1980.

Wilkinson-Latham, R. J.: *A Pictorial History of Swords and Bayonets.* London, 1973.

Wilson, H. W.: *Japan's Fight for Freedom* (the Russo-Japanese War). London, 1904–5.

Woodward, David: *Armies of the World 1854–1914.* Sidgwick & Jackson, London, 1978.

Yumoto, John M.: *The Samurai Sword.* Tuttle, 1958.

A naval officer, 1868.

A naval officer in full dress, 1874.

A naval officer, 1896.

A navy first lieutenant in battle dress, 1942.